From Head-Hunters to Church Planters

Revival simply means the action of the Holy Spirit in our lives. This action in a Christian's soul must always result in a definite change towards maturity. When a person is resuscitated, oxygen immediately enters the lungs and movement of the body starts. This is what the Holy Spirit does to a numb soul.

During my 20-year association with the revival movement, I have seen that continuous change is the heartbeat of revival. The mighty revival that broke out and swept across Nagaland was a wind of refreshing to the numb souls of Naga Christians.

Hevukhu Achumi Sema

From Head-Hunters to Church Planters

An Amazing Spiritual Awakening in Nagaland

Paul Hattaway

Authentic

Authentic Publishing
We welcome your comments and questions.
129 Mobilization Drive, Waynesboro, GA 30830 USA authentic@stl.org
and 9 Holdom Avenue, Bletchley, Milton Keynes, Bucks, MK1 1QR, UK
www.authenticbooks.com

If you would like a copy of our current catalog, contact us at:
1-8MORE-BOOKS
ordersusa@stl.org

From Head-Hunters to Church Planters
ISBN-10: 1-932805-71-0
ISBN-13: 978-1-932805-71-0

10 09 08 07 06 / 6 5 4 3 2 1

Published in 2006 by Authentic

Cover design: Projectluz
Cover photograph by Richard Diran. Used with permission. All rights reserved.
Interior design: TO A TEE, www.2at.com

Printed in the United States of America

Contents

Foreword

When I heard that my friend Paul Hattaway was writing a book on the revivals in Nagaland, I was thrilled. His previous books have been a great blessing to many Christians, in Nagaland and around the world. With God-given wisdom he has written down many of the Lord's mighty deeds, and as a result people have fasted and prayed, motivated and inspired to stir up God's gift inside them.

For countless centuries, the various tribes of the Nagas have inhabited the hilly regions between the River Brahmaputra in India and the River Chindwin in Myanmar (formerly Burma). It is fair to assume that we have been most famous around the world for our former practice of head-hunting. Many books have been written about this.

Of far more significance, however, is the story of how the Lord Jesus Christ has sent great and powerful revivals among us over the last 50 years. The message of God's salvation first reached our people in 1872, but it was only in the 1950s that large numbers of us came to know Christ as our wonderful personal Saviour. Today, almost one million Christians live joyful lives in Nagaland. We have been conquered by God's overwhelming grace and love. Many individual lives have been transformed by the revivals, and there has been greater lay participation in the church's total ministry as many have discovered their calling from God.

I recommend *From Head-Hunters to Church Planters* as an accurate and incisive account of what God has done among the Nagas. May he be glorified through this book, and may your own heart be revived as you read the wonderful things he has done in Nagaland!

Gwayhunlo Khing

Director of Asia Soul Winners and former pastor of
the Rengma Baptist Church, Kohima, Nagaland

Introduction

After more than a dozen years as a missionary in various parts of Asia, I was both surprised and delighted when I had my first opportunity to enter Nagaland, a small mountainous state in north-east India.

Most of my years in Christian ministry had been spent in places where the truth of the gospel had yet to make any visible impact, in societies where the name of Jesus Christ was almost unknown. Invariably, our work had been with tiny groups of faithful Christians surrounded by millions of Buddhists, Muslims or Hindus.

Suddenly I was in Nagaland. I knew in advance that the majority of Nagas were Christians, but I knew little about how their conversion had come about or how their faith had fared after so long in isolation. For the best part of 50 years, all but a handful of foreigners had been banned from entering the remote Naga Hills.

After I arrived in Kohima, the capital of Nagaland, I spent time with many Naga Christians, preaching in their churches, eating in their homes and getting to know them. I soon realized that I had met members of God's family, the Body of Christ, who reflected his beauty, humility, gentleness and faithfulness.

I started to wonder what kind of things could have happened among these people, a rare light in the midst of the overwhelming darkness in Asia. It is said that during the Naga revivals a person could drop a bundle of cash on the main street of Kohima and find it untouched the next day. The Nagas would never consider taking the money, as their lives were ruled by extreme reverence for a holy God.

As I came to learn later, the fruit of the Spirit that God has produced in the lives of nearly a million Naga Christians has come at great cost, through many severe trials and tests of their faith and commitment. On my very first visit to these beautiful people I realized that someone needed to record their story for the rest of the world to read. This is my feeble effort.

I have tried to set down faithfully what has been told to me by Nagas from many different tribes, as well as what I have learned from written accounts. I have included a number of first-hand testimonies from church leaders who experienced the power of God during remarkable visitations to their villages and homes in the 1950s, '60s and '70s.

There is a tendency today to associate 'revival' and miracles with charismatic churches, but there were none of those in Nagaland when God first brought revival there. These powerful and life-changing visitations came to orderly, conservative Baptist congregations. People who do not believe in miracles may pour scorn on some of the accounts in this book, but my challenge to them is simple: all of the names that appear in these pages are the actual names of real people, and all the places I mention are actual places. Readers can easily investigate for themselves by visiting these places and talking with the people, and can see and hear for themselves what happened when the Almighty God visited Nagaland.

I have also included a few testimonies of the kind of sufferings the Nagas have endured over the years as they have stood up for what they believed. My aim in telling just a handful of stories from those horrible years is not to distress and disgust the reader, nor to promote any particular political view. After much thought and prayer, I realized that in order to give an accurate account of revival among the Nagas I had to explain the circumstances that helped to prepare them to embrace Christ en masse.

I deeply appreciate the help I have received from many Naga church leaders, who eagerly agreed to be interviewed for this book. I think of the elderly Pastor Hopong of the Yimchung tribe, who walked through dense jungles and over high mountains for several days just to reach the nearest road, so that he and a co-worker could catch a bus to Kohima to see me. His commitment to tell the story of how God blessed his remote tribe is typical of many Nagas, who are determined to record the remarkable things Jesus Christ has done among their people in the last 50 years.

May the Lord Jesus Christ be glorified, and may his kingdom come throughout the whole world as it has among the Nagas!

Paul Hattaway

1

Who are the Nagas?

From one man [Adam] he made every nation of
men, that they should inhabit the whole earth;
and he determined the times set for them and the
exact places where they should live.

Acts 17:26

Nagas are a fine people, of whom their country is proud;
strong and self-reliant, with the free and independent
outlook characteristic of highlanders everywhere, good
to look at, with an unerring instinct of colour and design,
friendly and cheerful with a keen sense of humour, gifted
with splendid dances and a love of songs.

Elwin Verrier, *The Nagas in the Nineteenth Century*

As with all branches of the human race to survive since time
immemorial without a written script, the ancient history of the
Naga tribes of north-east India and western Myanmar (formerly
Burma) is shrouded in uncertainty. Some of them still have
oral stories, songs and poems recounting how their ancestors
originated in Central Asia. Their legends tell of harsh migrations
to the south, fleeing the oppression of the Chinese and hostile
tribes.

Other accounts tell how the Nagas were once 'rulers of the
oceans'. Even today, some of their women incorporate imported
conch and cowry shells in their traditional jewellery and dress,
even though the Naga Hills are situated hundreds of miles from
the nearest sea. Some scholars have noted the cultural similarities
between the Nagas and other head-hunting tribes such as the

Dayak and Kayan of Borneo, the Batak of Sumatra, the Igorot of the Philippines and various groups in Taiwan. All of these live near the sea.

The earliest reliable account placing the Nagas in their present location comes from the 13th century AD, when the Ahom, a Tai-speaking tribe, migrated into what is now north-east India. The historical records of their kings, the Borinjus, recount how the Ahom prince Sukhapa led his tribe through the Patkai Hills en route to modern-day Assam. They fought fierce battles with the Nagas, who had already settled in the hills, and many of the Ahom were killed.

Almost two millennia ago, around AD 150, the Greek scientist and scholar Claudius Ptolemy, in his Geographia, referred to the area north of modern-day Bangladesh as 'Nagaloi', meaning 'the realm of the naked'. Although it is true that the Naga people did go about unclothed, it is more likely that the primitive people described by Ptolemy are hardly related to today's Nagas. The name 'Naga' was given to these tribes by outsiders and just what it meant is open to much debate, with as many as a dozen different theories put forward by scholars.[1]

Linguists often hold the key to unlock uncertain histories of people groups. All the Naga languages are part of the Tibeto-Burman family, which consists of more than a thousand varieties spread from China, Tibet and Nepal to Vietnam and Laos in south-east Asia. The Nagas can be shown to be distant relatives of the eight million Yi people in southern China and the Akha of northern Thailand—now-fragmented groups that many centuries ago had more ethnic cohesion.

Undoubtedly, one of the main historical reasons for the disintegration of the Tibeto-Burman race into countless tribes was the invasion of south-west China by the Mongols in 1253. As their hordes advanced they slaughtered millions of people, often killing every living soul they came across. Many tribes and clans scattered to avoid certain death. Some hid in the mountains until the immediate danger had passed, but others travelled vast distances in search of a new land beyond the reach of the Mongol Empire.

It is likely that the ancestors of the Naga people left southern China in the 13th century, migrating first into modern-day Myanmar and then on into the rugged mountains that came to be known as Nagaland. This timing places them in their present homeland just before the first record of their existence, when the unfortunate Ahoms attempted to pass through their territory. Wherever the first Nagas came from, there is no doubt they have been living almost exclusively in their current locations for many centuries. Their oral traditions go back at least 52 generations.

When Westerners first came into regular contact with the Nagas in the 1800s, they found a fearsome people who practised head-hunting and yet were also a people of strong character and convictions, whose society and culture offered much to admire. John Henry Hutton wrote:

> Nagas have fine qualities. They are simple, humorous, courteous and hospitable. Nagas are people with a sense of humour and generosity at home, at work and at gatherings; laughter is the food of the society and hospitality is overwhelming. Nagas are honest and truthful people, stealing is not common . . . and they have respect for elders. . . . They are healthy, actively vigorous and brave people. The Nagas are well built and enthusiastically looking for a true God.[2]

The fact that most Nagas now find themselves living within the borders of India certainly doesn't mean they can in any way be associated historically, biologically, culturally, linguistically or ethnically with other Indian races. To this day, when a Naga needs to make a trip down onto the plains or to a large city such as Kolkata (formerly Calcutta), he will tell his friends and family that he needs to travel 'to India'. The implication is that the Nagas do not consider Nagaland to be part of India.

2

Hunting for Heads

When the cock first crows, the Nagas rush with great
shouting into the village and cut up everybody they meet
with, sparing neither old infirm men nor helpless women
nor children: even the cows, pigs and poultry of the foe
are slaughtered. Sometimes the victors remain on the
spot two or three days, but generally [they] return to their
own village on the same day, taking with them the heads,
hands and feet of those they have massacred: these they
parade about from house to house, accompanied with
drums and gongs, throwing liquor and rice on the heads
and uttering all manner of incantations. . . . They then
sing, dance and perform all manner of antics, pierce and
mangle the heads of their enemies, and again with curses
enjoin them to summon their whole race to suffer the
same ignominious treatment.

John Butler, 1847

Head-hunting was practised by the Nagas for so many centuries
that no one is quite sure how it began. It became such an intricate
and essential part of their culture and identity that no account of
these people could be complete without reference to it.

Many Westerners have wrongly assumed that head-hunting
was merely a matter of violence and murder, but for the pre-
Christian Nagas it was much more than that. To them, it was
something noble to be admired, a proof of bravery and strength.
The Naga historian Joseph Thong explains:

The practice of head-hunting and Feast of Merit are at
the heart and soul of the Naga culture, around which the
rest of the life activities are inter-woven. Establishment

of Village, the village gate, construction of house and its decorations, dress and ornaments, wood-carving, stone monuments, dyeing, tattooing, songs and dances, marriage, implements and tools, cultivation, chieftainship, clan system, beliefs, rituals and festivals etc revolve around and link up with head-hunting and Feast of Merit, which are basically the same in almost all the Naga tribes, except for some local and minor variations from tribe to tribe, village to village and clan to clan.[3]

The Nagas say they learned how to fight by watching ants raid each other's nests. In early times, one tribe or village waged war against another over land and other such subjects of dispute. When the war parties returned with stories of great victories and slaughters, some people remained unconvinced because they had only the word of the warriors for it. To substantiate their claims, the warriors therefore decided to bring home parts of their victims' bodies, such as their kneecaps. This practice gradually evolved into cutting off arms, but these proved too heavy to carry any great distance through the jungle.

Joseph Thong recounts:

One day, a warrior, while on his way to fight his enemies, saw two red ants fighting each other in the forest. As he watched the fight he saw one red ant had killed the other and severed its head, which was then carried into its hole. The warrior liked what he saw and started cutting off his victim's head whenever he made a kill. Others too started appreciating this idea, as carrying the head was handier. This was how the idea of beheading the dead victim started.[4]

When it came to head-hunting, gender and age did not matter. The only restrictions on a warrior were that he could not kill someone from the same clan or family, or anyone who was crippled or insane. Indeed, some Naga tribes accorded particular honour to warriors who returned with the heads of women and children, because they were usually protected in the heart of the village by the opposing fighters and to have slain them meant that the warrior must have performed an exceptional feat of bravery.

One contemporary Naga has even defended the culture of head-hunting by comparing it favourably with modern-day warfare. He argues that head-hunting is practised

> . . . all over the world. The so-called civilized countries wipe out the whole population of a certain area with chemical weapons and look down on another ethnic group for killing a few men with a simple tool and call it 'anarchism', whereas destroying millions of lives with chemical weapons is seen as a 'civilized, scientific and lawful act'.[5]

The same writer goes on to lament:

> Although some British colonial administrators, American Christian missionaries, travellers, journalists, military personnel, Naga national workers, church organizations, local administrators, academicians and other writers have written books on the Nagas, so far no comprehensive book covering the various aspects of the culture of the Naga head-hunters has been produced to meet the needs of those who hunt for [heads].[6]

According to another Naga source, the motivation for head-hunting among the Konyak tribe was one of love—'love for God and brotherly love for man. The highest offering and sacrifice a man could offer God was human blood. On all important occasions human blood was to be shed. This was done as a token of their love and gratitude to God'.[7]

It should be remembered that these twisted sentiments were expressed decades before any part of the Bible was translated into the Naga languages, and a generation or two before the consciences of the Naga people were awakened by the Holy Spirit.

When the British gained control of Naga territory, their plans to put a stop to head-hunting met with limited success. For example, on Christmas Day, 1909, a British officer went to Tuensang intent on punishing those who had been involved in a recent head-hunting raid. He ordered the village chiefs to hand over the men in question, but they replied, 'Does a hunter give away his hounds?'

The officer, seeing he would not get what he came for, then demanded payment of a fine for head-hunting. This time the reply was: 'We have no coins. We hear the government makes coins. If they are short, let them make some more.'[8]

The practice of head-hunting only started to subside after the gospel took hold and Naga Christians learned of the value God places on human life. Joseph Thong notes:

> The American Baptist missionaries played a vital role
> in bringing the head-hunting culture to an end, by
> convincing their converts that head-hunting is a sin and
> is against morality. God, the Creator of man and the
> universe, will punish those who murder their fellow men.
> Therefore, all who embraced Christianity automatically
> stopped head-hunting raids.[9]

Some of the last instances of head-hunting in Nagaland occurred during the Naga war with India. This led to some uncomfortable experiences for Naga Christians fighting alongside non-Christians who saw it as their duty to cut off their enemies' heads. On April 1, 1957, the Naga army triumphed in a battle at Dzüleikie:

> Next came the gruesome task of beheading some of the
> dead bodies so that their heads could be taken to their
> camps, where the victory ceremonies and rituals would
> be performed. Many turned away from this gory act,
> as there were among them some Christians who never
> participated in such rituals. But for the non-Christian
> this taking of heads back to their camps was a necessary
> part of their mission to ensure future victory and guard

against disastrous results in other missions. As they walked away from the scene of the day's battle, they turned around and addressed the dead, declaring, 'Your sin has been your undoing. The guilt is not upon me.'[10]

As tens of thousands of Nagas came into relationship with Christ in the 1960s and '70s, the practice of head-hunting faded into the pages of history. Only in the remote jungles of Myanmar, where some Konyak Nagas live in extremely isolated villages, is it still rumoured to continue today.

3

The First Christians

The late 18th century saw the beginning of the Protestant missionary enterprise. William Carey, later dubbed 'the father of modern missions', arrived in India in 1793, and was followed by the now legendary figures of Robert Morrison, who went to China in 1807, and Adoniram Judson, who introduced the gospel to Burma in 1813. The Khasi tribe in Assam had the honour of being the first ethnic group in north-east India to hear the gospel, when Krishna Chandra Pal, a convert of William Carey, led two Khasis to Christ in 1812.

Major Francis Jenkins, then Commissioner-General of Assam, first suggested the idea of missionaries coming to the remote hills of north-east India. He found that the tribespeople of the area were 'not only a nuisance, but treacherous and tricky demon-worshippers as well. The only thing that will make them better is Christianity.'[11] The British Baptists thought better of his invitation and decided that it would be more convenient for the American Baptists to go, given that they were already in the process of establishing a work in neighbouring Burma.

The Americans readily responded. The Rev Nathan Brown and the Rev O T Cutter and their wives set out from Calcutta on November 20, 1835 and reached Sadiya in Assam on March 23, 1836, after a gruelling four-month journey of 800 miles up the River Brahmaputra. Cyrus and Rhoda Bronson arrived a year later and moved to Jaipur, on the edge of the Naga Hills. There they were joined by the Browns and Cutters in May 1839, when they abandoned Sadiya after the British Colonel Adam White and eight others had been brutally killed by Khampti tribesmen.

These pioneer missionaries were of tough stock. They had forsaken all to follow the Saviour, and no hardship could prevent them from accomplishing their task. Bronson wrote to the Board of Missions:

> We want the choicest men the church has to consecrate; men well disciplined in mind—well versed in the study of human nature—of unfailing patience—possessing a zeal that difficulty will only enkindle; men who can press onward to the accomplishment of an object for years amid every sacrifice, and not faint; not self-willed, not high-minded, but ready to take any place appointed to them in the providence of God; above all, men of deep piety.[12]

Their strength of character was illustrated in the person of Edward Scott. When he visited the Makir tribe in Assam, the village chief and his warriors confronted him with spears and accused him of coming to steal their children and carry them away as slaves. With bulging eyes, they threatened the missionary with death if he advanced any further. Scott responded by calmly taking out his violin. With tears of joy, he sang the hymn

> Alas! and did my Saviour bleed
> And did my Sovereign die?
> Would he devote that sacred head
> For such a worm as I?

> Was it for crimes that I have done
> He groaned upon the tree?
> Amazing pity! grace unknown!
> And love beyond degree!

The warriors were both thrilled and amazed at the sound of the violin. Their threatening faces softened and no harm was done to Scott.

Although missionaries were labouring among other tribes in north-east India, the honour of being the first to bring the gospel to the Nagas belongs to Cyrus and Rhoda Bronson, who made two exploratory trips into their territory in 1839. On March 13, 1840, they moved to the Naga Hills and began working at Namsang. Just a few months later, however, their entire family was afflicted with severe illness and they were obliged to abandon their station and move back to Jaipur. They never returned, and the work at Namsang ceased. The missionary enterprise among the Nagas withdrew to the plains, and a Christian presence in the Hills remained an unfulfilled dream for the next seven years.

In 1847, Major John Butler wrote the following negative evaluation of the missionaries' prospects among the Nagas:

> The south-eastern hills of Assam are the abode of many tribes of Nagas. They are a very uncivilized race, with dark complexions, athletic sinewy frames, hideously wild and ugly visages: their faces and bodies being tattooed in a most frightful manner by pricking the juice of the bela nut into the skin in a variety of fantastic figures. They are reckless of human life; treacherously murdering their neighbours often without provocation, or at least for a trivial cause or offence. The greater number of Nagas are meant to be in a very destitute state, living almost without clothing of any kind. Their poverty renders them remarkably free from any prejudices in respect of diet: they will eat cows, dogs, cats, vermin, and even reptiles, and are very fond of intoxicating liquors.

> Amongst a people so thoroughly primitive, and so independent of religious prepossessions, we might reasonably expect missionary zeal would be most successful; for the last eight years, however, two or three American Baptist missionaries have in vain endeavoured to awake in them a sense of the saving virtues of Christianity. . . . In 1839, the missionaries turned their attention more particularly towards the Nagas; they took up their residence on the Boree Dehing River, at Jetpore [Jaipur], established a school, and were indefatigable in

endeavouring to gain some correct knowledge of the
savage tribes in their vicinity. A few years' experience
here proved the futility of their plans. Instead of
wandering amongst the savage tribes scattered over an
immense extent of country, in unhealthy, dense jungles,
it would have been prudent and politic to have afforded
instruction in the first instance to the populous villages in
the plains.[13]

The Baptist missionaries did indeed make contact with Nagas
from time to time on the Assam plains. Hube, a Konyak Naga,
is recorded to have been the very first Naga Christian. He was
baptized on September 12, 1847, but died a few weeks later, on
October 10.[14] The second was Longjanglepzuk, an Ao Naga from
the village of Merangkong. The Rev Francis Wayland baptized
him on September 7, 1851. About three years later, his village was
attacked by Konyak head-hunters and he was killed in the raid.

In 1855, two more Konyak men were baptized, named Aklong
and Amlai from the village of Namsamg. 'These men returned to
their village preaching the gospel of God. The leaders of the village
thought that the new religious teaching would create confusion
in the minds of the people and turn the village upside-down.
Therefore, for the sake of "peace and order" they exterminated
the two men.'[15]

Satan was doing all he could to crush the seed of the gospel
among the Nagas. The first four to become Christians were all
dead within a short time of their conversion to Christ. In Scripture,
we see that Satan often attempts to put a stop to God's planned
deliverances before they have a chance to get under way. When
Moses was born, Satan prevailed upon Pharaoh to command that
all newborn Israelite boys should be thrown into the River Nile
(Exodus 1:22). Similarly, when Jesus was born the jealous King
Herod ordered the massacre of all boys in Bethlehem under the
age of two (Matthew 2:16). But Satan's schemes were frustrated

on both these occasions, and his plan to strangle the Naga church in its infancy also turned out to be a dismal failure.

The Ao were the first of the Naga tribes to receive the gospel in significant numbers. In early 1871, an Ao man named Subongmeren from the village of Dekahaimong was making a trip to Sibsagar to trade when he came into contact with the missionary Dr E W Clark and an Assamese evangelist called Godhula. He believed on the Lord Jesus and was baptized.[16]

As Godhula listened to Subongmeren's stories about his community, a vision and desire grew in his heart to take the gospel to the rest of this man's tribe. As the missionary Dr S W Rivenburg wrote, he 'was a zealous man in the prime of his youth, yet he was willing to take the gospel to those wild barbarians whom Assamese generally disliked.'[17]

Clark had strictly warned Godhula never to go beyond the tea plantations that surrounded the mission compound in Sibsagar, because just beyond them lay the start of the Naga Hills, which he considered too dangerous to enter. But Godhula was convinced that God wanted him to take the gospel to the Nagas, so he disobeyed his employer. 'To go further meant a great risk. But [he] was ready for that risk and resolved to obey God rather than man.'[18]

The brave pioneer had already met and befriended a number of Nagas and they agreed to take him to their village, where he could meet the headman and request permission to stay. Two days later, they arrived at Dekahaimong. Godhula

> . . . explained the purpose of his visit and proclaimed the good news of Jesus Christ to the villagers. The village chiefs were not happy. They took him to be a British spy and imprisoned him for a few days. There he sung and prayed and the people began to come and stand around to listen to him. They became friendly and Godhula soon won the hearts of many. When he told them of his intention to return to Sibsagar, the people were sad. At

his departure, women and children wept. No less than
forty men escorted him to Sibsagar, thus paying him a
high honour. . . . Successful Christian ministry among the
Nagas was thus inaugurated by Godhula, the Assamese
evangelist.[19]

Godhula made several trips to Dekahaimong during the winter
of 1871/72, and on November 8, 1872, he led a group of Nagas to
Sibsagar to be baptized.

Nine men confessed their Christian experience before the
church and Clark baptized them on November 11. They were
registered as members of the Sibsagar Church for the time
being, since there was no church in the Naga Hills, but then they
returned to their village and built a chapel there. On December 18,
Clark, Godhula and other members of the Sibsagar Church made
a trip to Dekahaimong and five days later 15 men confessed their
Christian faith and were baptized. This was the first baptismal
service ever held in Nagaland and was the humble beginning of
the Naga church. In December 1972, that church celebrated its
centenary and commemorated that first baptism.[20]

As a result of inter-village tensions, on October 24, 1876 the
Christians of Dekahaimong decided to start a new community
on an uninhabited mountaintop about three miles to the west.
They named the new village Molungyimsen. 'Here in all the ages
was the first Naga village to hold Christ as King, all praise to his
name.'[21]

Considerable ill feeling arose when this new, Christian
village refused to sacrifice cattle during the great spirit festival
of the Ao, and for this and other reasons the village headman at
Dekahaimong decided to take action.

This meant a declaration of war. . . . Consequently a threat
came from the old village to exterminate the new village
and to take possession of the white man [E W Clark]'s
head as well. The Christians replied that the new village
very earnestly desired to live in peace and amity with

all others. They said, 'We are accepted disciples of the Almighty God, who made the earth and all in it, and who cares for his children.' They added, 'We trust in him and we beg that you be his friends and not foes.' Most earnest was the prayers. A peaceful message came. Christians praised the Lord.'[22]

It is difficult to imagine the courageous faith demanded of Clark, Godhula and the other Christian pioneers who first ventured into Naga territory with the gospel. The threat of decapitation was not an idle one. Beheading was frequent. As M M Clark wrote,

> Those were the days when people from other countries were afraid to go to the Naga Hills, because doing so could mean death and mutilation. . . . When Rev. Clark had gone to the Naga Hills, leaving his wife at Sibsagar, one British officer . . . asked Mrs. Clark, 'Have you heard from Mr. Clark? Do you ever expect to see your husband back with his head on his shoulders?'[23]

Satan did not gladly accept the introduction of Christianity to the hills that had been his unchallenged domain for centuries. Life for the small Naga Christian community was difficult. In 1887, the Rev Sidney Rivenburg reported, 'During the year we passed through much by which our lives were jeopardized; but through all God was better than our foolish ways. It has been a long time of severe trial to our church members. The horrors of savage warfare at our door required all the fortitude we all possessed to remain at our posts.'[24]

The missionaries were not merely tough Christians. Their courage stemmed from a deep love—first for Jesus Christ and second for the people they had come to reach. Note the longing expressed in this 1891 letter from Rivenburg:

> It has been my daily practice to go into the Naga village, and give out medicine to the sick, and preach to whomsoever would listen. My throat is not all right, and

from one to two hours talking has been about the limit of daily preaching. Hundreds have listened, and many with apparent interest. About two weeks ago I had the first sign. After having talked very earnestly for a long time to a company of very sober, interested listeners, one man said very solemnly, 'We will keep it.' How much the truth had really taken hold of his heart, I do not know. But this I know: in the four long years I have not heard as much from heathen lips before. I long to see some souls saved. The lack of converts greatly depresses me.[25]

And so, through the brave efforts of a few sanctified men and women, the fire of the gospel was lit in Nagaland. At first, it was a mere flicker that looked ready to be snuffed out. Decades of laborious effort had produced meagre results: by 1911, after 71 years of missionary work, the number of Naga Christians totalled just 1,128. But over the years the fire burned brighter and brighter, clearing the ground for the incredible events that were to follow generations later.

4

The Gospel Takes Root

In Nagaland today live 13 distinct tribes of Naga people.[26] They are differentiated from each other by language, dress and customs, yet they are also bound together by a common history and a broad ethnic identity.

In this chapter, we briefly study how the gospel first took hold among each tribe, preparing the way for the powerful revivals that followed in the 1950s, '60s and '70s. We examine each tribe in chronological order of its Christianization, from the Ao, amongst whom the first Naga church was established in 1872, all the way down to the Yimchung, who saw their first convert to Christ baptized a full eighty years later.

The Ao Nagas

The Ao are the most populous tribe in Nagaland today, numbering approximately 150,000. As recounted in the previous chapter, this was the first Naga tribe to experience a significant turning to Christ. The church grew slowly but steadily, until in 1885 the pioneer missionary E W Clark reported that a revival had begun at Molung. It was still continuing four years later. In 1898 alone, 104 Ao were baptized. Converts were added to the church every year into the early 1900s, largely because of the Christian schools that the missionaries had established. By 1905, the church had 685 members.

In 1913, the awakening gathered momentum as lay preachers travelled to every Ao village and preached the salvation of Christ. By 1920, there were 46 Ao churches, with 3,838 members. The Ao sent missionaries to neighbouring tribes such as the Lotha,

Sumi, Chang and Konyak, and great things happened as Christ conquered the hearts of thousands and the grip of sin and violence began to loosen. By 1930, the Ao church was self-supporting. Altogether, there were 9,000 Christians, of whom 7,000 had full church membership.

The advance of the Kingdom of God among the Ao was now poised for the phenomenal revival of the 1950s. It is remarkable to think that the Ao church had begun only because a faithful Christian named Godhula had chosen to disobey the orders of his missionary employers and ventured into the Naga Hills with the message of salvation.

The Lotha Nagas

The Lotha Nagas today number around 80,000 people in west central Nagaland, around the town of Wokha.

The good news of Jesus Christ first arrived among them through the influence of Christian schools and Sunday schools established by the American Baptist missionaries. Initial attempts to reach the Lotha were not very encouraging at all. The first conversion occurred in the 1880s, but most people proved extremely resistant to efforts to evangelize them.

The strategy of reaching people through Christian education—which later proved successful among other Naga tribes—at first did not work with the Lotha. On September 18, 1886, the missionary W E Witter wrote:

> The school problem is most perplexing. To get these
> savages to attend school, we must at least give them
> their rice; for the parents have as yet no desire that their
> children be taught to read and write, and would as soon
> throw their rice in the fire as send it to the station for the
> support of a boy in school.[27]

On one occasion, Witter told the Lotha students that if they studied diligently they might be able to further their studies in another country when they were older. Many parents promptly withdrew their children from the school, afraid that they would never see them again.

However, although there was little to show for the first 20 years of evangelism, good seed was being sown for a large harvest in years to come. What began as a trickle of converts soon became a steady flow, and then a powerful stream. Even the beleaguered Christian schools started to produce results. In 1904, the missionaries reported:

> The Lotha work is perhaps the most encouraging part of the work. Boys have been drawn from every part of that tribe for the training school. Good numbers have become Christians. The past year a fairly strong church has been built up at Okotso village.[28]

The 1920s saw the Lotha church well and truly established. In 1921, it had only 149 members, but two evangelists named Ibansao and Chichamo boldly proclaimed the gospel to their fellow tribesmen and within just one year its membership increased to 257. Throughout the decade, more than a hundred baptisms were recorded every year. In 1929, Ibansao baptized 168 converts, bringing the total membership to 758. And within another seven years the church had more than doubled to 1,789 baptized believers meeting in 37 congregations.[29]

The numbers rose every year, and by 1946 the Christian community had increased to over half of the total population. The translation and printing of the Lotha New Testament in 1944 contributed greatly to the numerical and spiritual growth of the church, as hungry believers read God's word in their own language for the first time.

The Lotha church had come a long way since 1886, when Witter had lamented, 'To get these savages to attend school, we must at least give them their rice.'

The Angami Nagas

Today, more than 90,000 Angami Nagas live in western Nagaland and parts of the Indian state of Manipur.

While the gospel had started to take root among the Ao and other Naga tribes in the late 1800s, the Angami near Kohima (the capital of Nagaland) proved stony ground for the Christian message. C D King and his wife, Anna, were the first missionaries appointed to reach them, in 1879. It was later reported:

> The response of the Angami was not like that of the Ao or any other tribes in Nagaland. It was slow. Angami seemed to be more resistant to change, whether political, social or religious. Samaguting was the first Angami village to host the Kings but it was the last to receive Christ.[30]

The first Angami Christian was a man named Sieliezhü, who was baptized on June 21, 1885. By 1906, the total number of Christians in this tribe was just 35.

The following years saw church membership fluctuate as a number of people backslid. The missionaries had their hands full dealing with problems of church discipline. Of C D King's first four converts, one was excommunicated for worshipping spirits and another for adultery. In 1910, the Angami church had 90 members. In 1914, it had 151, in 1918 248—then back down to 212 in 1920.[31]

However, the arrival of the missionaries Mr and Mrs George Supplee in 1922 greatly strengthened the work in Kohima. In the following year, church membership doubled. Within five years, the Angami New Testament was completed, and in that same year, 1927, 455 people were converted to Christ and baptized. The Angami church had taken root and was slowly gaining in strength. By 1937, church membership in the Kohima area had grown by 1,736—of whom 630 were Angami.[32]

The Chakhesang Nagas

There are several distinct phases in the story of how God reached the Chakhesang Nagas. The name 'Chakhesang' is actually a condensation of the names of three allied tribes: the Chakrü, the Khezha and the Sangtam. Together these three sub-tribes total about 85,000 people in eastern and south-eastern Nagaland. Most numerous are the Sangtams (40,000), followed by the Khezhas (24,000) and the Chakrüs (21,000).

The gospel was first preached to the Chakhesang by Sidney Rivenburg in 1895. He and his wife, Hattie, had arrived in India in 1883 and they enjoyed a long and fruitful career as missionaries until 1923.[33]

After Sidney Rivenburg and two Naga evangelists named Sieliezhü and Kruneizhü first went to Chakhesang territory in 1895, a small congregation emerged in the village of Chazuba, about 40 miles east of Kohima. Many decades later, a 97-year-old man named Pushoyi recalled that first visit:

> Rivenburg requested the villagers to set up a thatched tabernacle for a gathering. They collected jungle materials and completed the tabernacle immediately. The meeting hall was attached to the house of Tazüho, the village chief. Rivenburg called a meeting and many people turned up. He preached about 'God the Creator' and 'a sure place of rest after death'. The preaching was translated by Kruneizhü. Sieliezhü was singing most of the time. People were listening to the message with great interest. They were there with their rice-beer cups in their hands in the manner of their traditional social gatherings. On the same day, ten persons accepted the Christian faith. There was no opposition or reaction. But later on, due to social pressure, seven out of the ten persons reverted to their former faith. The remaining three persons became the initial pillars and the Church began to grow with them.[34]

One factor that contributed to this immediate initial success seems to have been some prophecies uttered several hundred years before by a Chakhesang seer named Khamhimütülü. One church leader noted: 'She prophesied many future events, and her sayings are coming true. Her teachings are found to coincide with those of the Bible.'[35]

All the same, new converts faced strong opposition from their fellow tribesmen, who equated acceptance of Christianity with a betrayal of Chakhesang culture and history. Nonetheless, many of the believers stood firm in their faith and some—notably, three men named Sülüho, Lhüprüve and Sare—faithfully shared the gospel.

The Kuki Nagas

The Kuki Nagas today number more than 150,000 people spread across five states of north-east India. Approximately 80,000 live in Nagaland, and a further 26,200 inhabit neighbouring areas of Myanmar. Linguistically, the Kuki are rather distinct from other Naga tribes, with a language more closely related to the Chin languages of Myanmar than to other Naga varieties.

The gospel was first proclaimed among the Kuki in 1897, and it was commonly believed that the first baptism took place in 1908. However, when a stone inscription commemorating the 50th anniversary of the Kuki Baptist Association in Nagaland was unveiled, it stated: 'The late Mr. Ngulhao Thomsong was the first to be converted to Christianity in 1897.' Ngulhao was an early convert who left for Manipur, where he spent the rest of his life preaching and translating the Scriptures. Consequently, because he was not seen in Nagaland after his conversion, he was not widely recognized as the first Kuki Christian.

The first Kuki congregation was established at Sirhima on February 7, 1912. The church remained small and ineffective until an awakening in 1916 that resulted in the transformation of dozens of lives and a consequent expansion in church membership. Seventy-six people were baptized that year. 'With this, the non-Christian opposition was heightened to a great extent. They wanted to kill the Christians of the village. When Christians could no longer bear the threat and persecution they built a new village at Chalkot.'[36]

In 1936, there were still only 200 Kuki Christians in Nagaland. By 1950, this number had grown to 700, in 29 churches.

The Zeliangrong Nagas

'Zeliangrong' is a condensation of the names of three related tribes: the Zemes, the Liangmais and the Rongmeis. Together they number approximately 30,000 people, of whom most live in Nagaland but some inhabit communities in the Indian states of Manipur and Assam.

Christianity first came to the Zeliangrong Nagas when Angami evangelists visited them in the early 1900s. Three students of the Kohima Mission Training School were baptized on December 31, 1905, and among them was the headman of a Zeliangrong village, who is believed to have been the first Christian from his tribe.[37] For years, however, the Zeliangrong were resistant to the gospel and threatened those who tried to bring it to them.

By 1951, almost half a century after the light of the gospel first shone in their midst, the Zeliangrong church numbered a mere 80. In that same year, H K Lungalang, a Zeliangrong, resigned from his government job to dedicate his energies to preaching the gospel among his fellow tribesmen. In 1953, the Zeliangrong Baptists formed their own association and a spurt of growth occurred. By the end of 1955, there were 21 congregations, with 637 baptized Christians. By 1959, church membership stood at over a thousand.

The Sumi Nagas

The Sumi (or Sema) Nagas are one of the largest of the 13 tribes. Today, they number some 140,000 people, inhabiting parts of central and southern Nagaland.

The gospel first reached them in the early 1900s, when evangelists from the Ao, Angami and Lotha took the responsibility to reach out to their neighbours. The first Sumi Christian is reputed to have been a man named Ivilho of the village of Ghokimi, who was baptized in 1906. Ivilho and another Sumi named Jekique proved to be powerful evangelists, enduring great hardship for the gospel. One historian notes that, 'despite resistance, threats, persecution, and fines imposed on them, the Sumi were coming forth as professed Christians from different villages.'[38]

In the early years of the Sumi church, an entire village converted to Christ after an undeniable miracle occurred. A Sumi woman had been seriously ill for some time and was knocking on death's door.

> All their tribal efforts failed to heal her. Finally she was
> left to the Christians' God. It was their decision that, if
> she became well by praying to the God of the Christians,
> the whole village would become Christian. God answered
> the prayer. The woman was healed. This decisive event
> itself persuaded the whole village to profess Christianity
> as the true religion.[39]

This mass conversion brought extreme persecution from non-Christians in the surrounding areas, but the believers would not be swayed from their new convictions. As one writer later observed: 'Without the work of a missionary or the preaching of a native evangelist, [Sumi] people became Christians and organized themselves into churches.'[40]

By 1929, the total number of Sumi church members was 3,000. That same year, a dramatic conversion took place. A man named Inaho, who was a translator at the Mokokchung Court, had been a powerful enemy of Christ and a persecutor of Christians. When his father fell seriously ill, 'it was a time for Inaho to think. Christ spoke to him and he realized that there was no salvation outside Christ. He left his government job and entered into the ministry as an evangelist.'[41]

By 1936, there were 6,500 Sumi Christians. Just three years later, in 1939, the Baptists recorded 78 Sumi churches, with 8,000 members. A decade later, that number had swollen to 16,000 baptized believers in 150 congregations. However, despite these impressive figures, all was not well in the Sumi church. As one report lamented:

> Spirit worship, polygamy, drinking of rice beer and other evils threatened and undermined the good work for Christ. In 1951, 115 persons were expelled and 145 Christians reverted. Yet the number of the churches increased to 222 and the membership to 16,422.[42]

The Rengma Nagas

The Rengma number approximately 22,000 people today, located in central and western areas of Nagaland. They are the least numerous of the 13 Naga tribes.

The gospel first made an impact among the Rengma in 1918. The first convert was a spirit priest (or 'witchdoctor') named Phenuga Kemp. Kemp had been zealous for his ancient pagan religion, but after his first two daughters died he became sceptical about its efficacy and started searching for the truth. At that time he was informed that an Angami evangelist named Sieliezhü was preaching a new religion about a Supreme God who was more powerful than any demon. Kemp was so convinced of the truth of the gospel that he abandoned his spirit worship, destroyed the tools of his trade and wholeheartedly followed Jesus Christ.

The gospel was generally viewed with deep suspicion until 1922–23, when a large number of people were converted and baptized. By 1937, there were 350 Rengma Christians. The very next year, a further 114 were baptized. The church continued to grow steadily, albeit less spectacularly, among this tribe.

In 1950, the Rengma church had 1,300 members meeting in 13 congregations. Today, around 90 per cent of all Rengma are believers. When Phenuga Kemp, the witchdoctor, became the first Rengma Christian in 1918, nobody could have guessed that God would do such a tremendous work among this precious tribe.

The Konyak Nagas

The Konyak are one of the most easily recognizable Naga tribes. Their appearance is striking, with the men decorating their heads with huge tusks from wild boars. More than 120,000 Konyak are located in eastern Nagaland and a similar number spill across the border into western Myanmar. These combined populations make the Konyak the largest Naga tribe.

They also were the last of the Nagas to abandon head-hunting (though it is rumoured that isolated instances still take place in remote villages in Myanmar), and the last to experience the power of God's revival. It is somewhat ironic that (as recorded in the previous chapter) this tribe can also lay claim to the honour of the first known Naga Christian, the man named Hube who was baptized in 1847 but died less than a month later.[43]

For almost a century after that, the gospel struggled to make any inroads among the Konyak as the tribe gradually slipped into moral and spiritual decline. The growth of the church was painfully slow and fraught with difficulty. By 1940, its total membership in Nagaland was only 145. However, new programmes were launched by other Naga Christians to evangelize the Konyak and by the end of 1949 that figure had increased to 1,600.

When the Naga missionary Longri Ao first visited the Konyak in the village of Wakching in 1950, he reported:

> You should see the people . . . there is much sickness, they have no education. They are always afraid, even of each

other, because of head-hunting raids. Their chiefs are cruel, demanding tribute from all the villagers. Above all, they live in constant dread of their priests. Many of the villagers are completely naked; they suffer from cold and hunger.[44]

Longri did not just describe the dire state of the tribe to his fellow Christians, he was willing to do something about it. In 1950, he was among the delegates at a meeting to draft the constitution for the Council of Baptist Churches in Assam and he urged his fellow workers to look forward:

A great day is ahead for the Church in our land. We have endless opportunities for witnessing. . . . We must take up the task of the mission carried so long by the missionaries. There are people everywhere who still have not heard the name of Christ. We must witness or die. . . . A whole tribe is waiting for the light of the gospel. It is a difficult field. After all these years there is only a handful of Christians. If this council will send us, my family and I are ready to go to the Konyak as missionaries.[45]

When Longri and his wife first arrived in Wakching, they found that the few Christian families had been threatened with dire consequences if they refused to participate in their community's heathen religious ceremonies.

One afternoon a rumour spread that the Christians had openly defied the demand of the village and showed disrespect to the sacred spirits. The news had an instant result. An angry mob soon gathered and . . . rushed down towards the church, broke open the doors and damaged the church building and took away the church bell.[46]

The bell was thrown into a blazing fire. People had been particularly upset by its ringing because they believed the noise angered the spiritual guardians of the village.

However, God's plans were in no way hindered by such opposition and revival broke out in many places. Just a few months after the burning of the bell, more than 70 of the Konyak who had taken part in the raid on the church accepted Christ.

The Phom Nagas

Inhabiting many villages in north-eastern Nagaland around the town of Tuensang, the Phom Nagas today number roughly 35,000.

An Ao evangelist named Kijungluba is widely recognized as the earthen vessel God chose to first take the gospel to this tribe. The first Phom Christian was Imkum, of the village of Kaching, who was baptized in 1936. His son Mengkham went to Impur to receive Bible training and subsequently returned as the first Phom evangelist to his people.

Unlike their counterparts in most of the other tribes, the Phom Christians did not meet with much persecution. The new believers were able to continue to live in their villages and interact with other members of their families. As a result, the gospel spread and gradually more souls were gathered into the Kingdom of God. In 1943, the missionary C E Hunter wrote:

> Christ has claimed his first converts across the border.
> Only a few villages, but villages are large, some of them
> having about 600 houses. Ten people were baptized from
> one of these villages. . . . Head-hunting continued until
> a few years ago between this and a neighbouring village.
> The converts live among the wild people.[47]

By 1952, the Phom church had grown to 1,166 baptized members meeting in 12 congregations—though grounding the new believers in the word of God was difficult, as only 46 of them were literate at the time.

The Chang Nagas

More than 31,000 members of the Chang tribe live in parts of east central Nagaland, especially in Tuensang District, with further communities located in the Indian state of Assam.

The gospel was first preached to the Chang in the early 1900s, with little success. Their close-knit communities refused to allow any evangelists to visit them. They built a spiritual wall around themselves and were determined that it should not be penetrated. After the word of God reached the Ao village of Akhoia in 1906, it was hoped that the Ao would soon spread it to the Chang village of Yaongyimti just a short distance away, but the tribe's stubborn resistance meant that it was more than 30 years before the first of them believed.

The establishment of God's church among the Chang was greatly assisted by the ministry of an Ao evangelist, Onen Lepten Ao. A Chang man named Loyim was converted on September 5, 1937. He dared to go against his own culture in order to be counted as a child of God. Others soon followed. Persecution of the new believers was extreme. The Naga historian Phuveyi Dozo commented, 'The Chang are a warlike tribe. For years they were deadly against the gospel. Persecution of the few who became Christians was extreme—to the extent of killing the Christians.'[48]

Nonetheless, a church was built at Yaongyimti in 1940 to accommodate 50 worshippers. A key Chang leader named Imlong was enthusiastic in preaching the gospel to his fellow tribesmen, and he also translated the Gospel of Mark into their language in 1946. Four years later, the fire of the gospel started to spread among the Chang. By 1952, there were 21 churches with 1,573 members. By 1955, there were 2,915 baptized Christians, and by 1967 4,667, in 37 churches.

This small tribe, who had declared themselves enemies of the gospel, were finally conquered by the love of Christ. The sounds of praise and worship can today be heard in villages that once killed Christians.

The Khiamngan Nagas

Twenty-five thousand Khiamngan (or Khiamniungan) Nagas inhabit the eastern part of Tuensang District in Nagaland. Other communities are located across the border in Myanmar. This is perhaps the most inaccessible of all the tribes in Nagaland. Visiting their villages can mean several days' walk over high mountains and through deep valleys.

The practice of head-hunting exerted a powerful influence over the Khiamngan for much longer than most of the other Naga tribes. Consequently, the seed of the gospel only started to germinate among them in 1950, when a graduate of the Jorhat Bible School called Jongpong Wati went to live in the region. He learned the Khiamngan language and found the people eager to listen to the gospel. Soon the first of them put their trust in Jesus. The historian Puthuvail Philip recorded:

> The grace and mercy of God was shown to this people.
> They began to realize that their way of life was not the
> only way. Many began to confess Christ. In 1952, five
> churches were established. Their membership at the
> time was 410 persons. Only one church had a pastor.
> Membership rose to 538 and seventeen churches had
> been organized at the end of the year 1955. . . . The
> church grew from strength to strength each year as more
> villages and more people were won for Christ. The active
> Christian work continued and other tribal churches
> extended their help through prayer, personnel and
> financial support for the expansion of the church in that
> part of Nagaland.[49]

By 1967, the Khiamngan church numbered more than 5,000 members, among them many former head-hunters who had found God's abundant pardon at the foot of the Cross.

Jongpong Wati in 1950 was the first to take the gospel to the Khiamngan. He courageously walked alone into a tribe notorious for cutting off human heads, because he knew that God loved this tribe and desired them to be his children. Today, these people have been completely transformed. The hills and valleys that once were filled with sounds of grief and despair after head-hunting raids are now full of voices praising Jesus Christ.

The Yimchung Nagas

The Yimchung Nagas (also known as Yimchungrü) are also among the most remote and inaccessible of the tribes. There are still many tigers and bears roaming the rugged area where they live, and in consequence the gospel reached them much later than many other Naga groups. Hopong, a Yimchung pastor, told me:

> It is strange that some people ask us if our communities are becoming Westernized, because very few of our people have ever seen a Westerner before. Very, very few have ever ventured into our part of Nagaland. In fact, our Yimchung people do not even understand how a human being could be white. It doesn't make sense to them and they think we are joking when we say we have seen white people![50]

Today, there are some 35,000 Yimchung inhabiting 78 villages in northern Nagaland.

Sincere Ao and Sumi evangelists risked their lives to take the gospel to the Yimchung in 1950, at a time when head-hunting was rife among this tribe. In 1952, the first convert, a man named Mongo, received baptism, and several others followed soon after. As soon as Mongo's baptism took place,

> . . . the non-Christians became antagonistic. They compelled Mongo and the other Christians in the village either to leave or deny Christ. Some left the village; others denied Christ. Mongo reaffirmed his faith in Christ. . . . He, his wife and his children were all slain for their disobedience. It was not in vain. Later the villagers

were impressed by the cause for which Mongo stood. They found something extraordinary in the behaviour of Mongo and his family and after-thoughts led many to Christ.[51]

By 1958, the membership of the Yimchung church totalled 500. Rapid growth thereafter meant that by the end of 1960 there were 1,056 baptized believers, an increase of over 100 per cent in just two years.

Through decades of toil and perseverance, the seed of the gospel had finally begun to take root among all the tribes in Nagaland.

5

Betrayed by the British

The 19th century witnessed the expansion of colonial power throughout the world. The British came and administered Nagaland for 66 years,[52] making Kohima their regional headquarters in 1878. The annexation of the rest of Nagaland was a gradual process. However, although Nagaland was included in maps of the Empire as a conquered territory, 'it is correct to say that the British never had any absolute control of the Nagas. Inter-village feuds and head-hunting continued as before. . . . To a great extent the British left the Nagas to themselves.'[53] The British felt that the imposition of law and order on Nagaland would be too much trouble and expense. For their part, the Nagas were glad to be left alone. As long as the presence of the foreigners did not encroach on their freedom and dignity, they were content— though they also came to appreciate many of the social benefits the British brought to their communities.

In 1944, many Nagas fought alongside the British and Indians in the crucial Battle of Kohima, which finally stopped the Japanese in their tracks and thwarted their plans to invade and colonize India. Few Westerners have ever heard of this battle, yet it ranks alongside Midway, El Alamein and Stalingrad as one of the turning-points of the Second World War. Indeed, Lord Mountbatten described it as 'one of the greatest battles in history.'[54] The British Field Marshal Sir William Slim lauded the Naga contribution:

> There were gallant Nagas whose loyalty even in the most depressing times of the invasion has never faltered.
> Despite floggings, torture, execution and the burning

of their villages, they refused to aid the Japanese in any way or to betray our troops. Their active help to us was beyond the value of praise. Under the leadership of devoted British political officers they guided our columns, collected information, ambushed enemy patrols, carried our supplies, and brought in our wounded under the heaviest fire—and then, being the gentlemen they were, often refused all payment. Many a British and Indian soldier owes his life to the naked, head-hunting Naga, and no soldier of the Fourteenth Army who met them will ever think of them but with admiration and affection.[55]

The Nagas' struggle for independence began in earnest in 1929, when a written memorandum from the Naga Club was submitted to the Simon Commission. The 20 tribal leaders who were signatories to this document were deeply concerned to learn that their territory had been included in the Reform Scheme of India, a British initiative launched without any consultation with the Nagas.

In part, the memorandum stated:

Though our land at present is within the British territory, [the British] Government has always recognized our private rights in it, but if we are forced to enter the council of the majority all these rights may be extinguished by unsympathetic council. . . . If the British Government, however, wants to throw us away, we pray that we should not be thrust to the mercy of the [Indians,] who could never have conquered us themselves, and to who we are never subjected, but leave us alone to determine for ourselves as in ancient times.

No firm decision was made by the British, despite repeated declarations of independence and autonomy by the Nagas. With growing dissatisfaction with colonial rule spreading all across India, they were far too busy to deal with the Nagas' claims.

After the war, it became clear that British rule in India was drawing to a conclusion. This worried the Nagas, who feared that they could be betrayed and forgotten by their British friends. In 1947, they issued another memorandum, addressed to the departing British as well as the incoming Indian government. In it, they asked for the setting up of 'an Interim government for a period of ten years, at the end of which the Naga people will be left to choose any form of Government under which they will live'.

This and other urgent letters were sent to senior British politicians, including Sir Winston Churchill, who they hoped would come to their aid. Part of a letter sent to the House of Lords read:

> No argument is needed to show the Nagas are a separate
> people with their own customs, traditions and culture;
> and to say that the British Government has decided
> to hand over to Indian hands complete authority for
> governing of even Nagaland, in complete inconsistency
> with the policy of administration hitherto followed in the
> hills and in violation of implied but clear pledges during
> the past years, without even asking the opinion of the
> Nagas, is not only unjust but immoral.[56]

But the British continued to pay little attention to the Nagas, who had willingly spilled their blood to help repel the Japanese just a few years earlier.

Britain then proposed a scheme whereby the Nagas would join other tribal peoples of north-east India and Burma to form a territory that would continue under British rule even after the rest of India had gained its independence. This suggestion was rejected by the Nagas, who demanded complete sovereignty and self-determination. They did not want the option of continuing for a further 50 or 100 years under foreign dominion. Quite simply, they saw no possibility of compromise. They had always been free and they wanted to continue to be free. A firm line was drawn in the sand—but they were demanding something the Indians would not give them and the British seemed unwilling to.

On July 9, 1947, a delegation of nine Naga leaders travelled to New Delhi to meet Mahatma Gandhi. They stated their case for independence and made it clear that they would rather die than join the Indian Union. According to Naga sources, Gandhi assured them that they had every right to be independent if they wanted to be. One report said:

> When the Naga delegates pointed out that the Assam Governor, Sir Akbar Hydari, had threatened to use force against the Nagas in case they refused to join the Indian Union, Gandhi exclaimed, 'Sir Akbar is wrong. He cannot do that. . . . I will come to the Naga Hills; I will ask them to shoot me first before one Naga is shot.'[57]

Soon after this meeting, Gandhi was assassinated and the future of Nagaland began to look much bleaker.

Gandhi's successor, Jawaharlal Nehru, received numerous letters and delegations from Nagaland in the years after Indian independence, but all petitions fell on deaf ears. A referendum was held in Nagaland in which 99.9 per cent of the Naga people rejected the Indian constitution and demanded complete independence from Indian rule. The Nagas went ahead and declared independence, raising their own flag above their towns and villages. For a while, India seemed preoccupied with other matters and made no move against them.

When the Naga delegation visited Nehru in Delhi on March 11, 1952, they again stated their independence and told him of the results of the referendum. Nehru reportedly

> . . . exploded with anger, and banging his fists on the table he said, 'Whether heaven falls or India goes to pieces and blood runs red in the country, I don't care. Whether I am here or for that matter any other body comes in, I don't care. Nagas will not be allowed to become independent!'[58]

6

1955: Hell Comes to Nagaland

> To the church, a revival means humiliation, a bitter
> knowledge of unworthiness. . . . It is not the easy and
> glorious thing many think it to be. . . . It comes to scorch
> before it heals; it comes to condemn ministers and people
> for their unfaithful witness, for their selfish living, for
> their neglect of the Cross. . . . That is why a revival has
> ever been unpopular with large numbers within the
> church.
>
> James Burns

These days, whenever armed conflict erupts in the world it is
broadcast within hours via satellite television networks such as
CNN or the BBC. Fifty years ago, when hell came to Nagaland,
the Nagas were afforded no such exposure. A brutal war began in
earnest in 1955 between the massive forces of the Indian Army
and the Nagas: a war that few outsiders knew about, because it
took place in the remote and isolated Naga Hills, with no reporters
present. This war has continued for half a century, interrupted by
occasional ceasefires.

The Naga Christians did not ask for a war with India, and
they did not want to be involved in the taking of human life. Yet
many felt they were compelled to fight in self-defence against the
incredible onslaught they faced. As you read this chapter you may
come to understand that the intention of the Indian government
was nothing short of the complete annihilation of the Naga
people. Its troops did not come to make or keep peace, or even
to force a surrender. They came to pillage, rape and massacre as
many Nagas as possible—soldiers or civilians, male or female,
elderly or infants, it didn't matter.

Some of the most brutal conflicts in history have been triggered by some cultural offence, and this is true of the war between India and the Nagas. The Indian government announced that the Prime Minister, Jawaharlal Nehru, would visit Kohima on March 30, 1953. The Prime Minister of Burma, U Nu, would also be present, at a meeting where the future of Nagaland was to be discussed. The Nagas welcomed the presence of the two premiers, hoping that one last effort could be made to achieve the complete independence they desired.

On the appointed morning, about 15,000 Nagas assembled in Kohima to give a warm welcome to the two prime ministers. Just 10 minutes before the meeting was due to begin, however, the Indian side announced that no written or spoken submission from the Nagas would be allowed, and no questions could be asked.

In Naga culture, such a demand seemed grievous and disgraceful. One Naga writer explains:

> To be told that a . . . guest would not talk to his hosts was simply unbelievable to the Nagas. As a result, the hosts as one man rose and walked out of the public meeting place—the outdoor stadium at Kohima. Nehru and U Nu were left to address only a handful of Government servants.

> This was a most humiliating experience for Nehru, who had never ever experienced anything like this in his whole public life. Immediately following this incident, arrest warrants were issued against eight Naga leaders. . . . Following the raids on houses of Naga leaders, many went into hiding. The Assam police and paramilitary forces began to arrest many people at random. Properties of leaders were confiscated and auctioned, crops in the fields were destroyed and wives and children of several leaders were arrested and detained in jails.

> There were also unfounded charges that American missionaries were behind the movement, and all

American Baptist missionaries were driven away from Nagaland. . . . Things began to move at a very fast pace.[59]

During 1954, the Indian hatred of the Nagas intensified to such a degree that full-scale war became inevitable. The Indians, mostly Hindus, considered the tribespeople the worst kind of scum, not worthy of their attention. The caste system that is responsible for many of the social ills prevalent in India categorizes tribal people as lower than animals. For the Nagas to show such stubborn insolence to the face of the Indian government for so long was more than India could take. When the cauldron boiled over, the result was of such a demonic savagery that only Satan himself and the hosts of hell could have conjured up the fury that was vented on the Nagas.

On March 31, 1955, the Naga National Council sent the following telegraph to the United Nations:

> Reports reaching Kohima say that more than ten thousand men, women and children of Free Nagas are believed to have been already killed by the Indian troops within the last few days of wholesale massacre. People are being butchered systematically from village to village in Free Nagaland. We urgently appeal to you in the name of humanity to intervene and stop the killings.

The UN failed to respond.

The Naga people, proud and free, had been betrayed by the British they had so loyally served and were now forsaken by the rest of the world. They were left to face the military might of India alone.

Six months after the NNC's telegraph reached the UN, the Indian Army moved into Nagaland officially with two divisions, and 'the horror and nightmare of Nagaland multiplied a hundredfold.'[60] Thousands of people were slaughtered like helpless animals. It made no difference whether the victims were combatants or civilians, men, women, children or babies.

Such distinctions meant nothing to the Indian soldiers. Their enemy was anyone unfortunate enough to be born a Naga. What occurred was what, much later, was to become euphemistically known as 'ethnic cleansing'. The Indians seemed determined to erase the Naga people from the face of the earth.

The woeful experiences of the Nagas are too many to document and too horrible to read. I hope it will suffice to relate a few brief stories here, of a handful of Nagas among the thousands killed by Indian troops in the first year of their occupation . . .

On June 6, 1956, Mr Solomon, a member of the Ao Naga Church Council, and Deacon Imtilepzuk were tied to posts along with four other Christians in the village of Longpha and publicly executed by firing squad.

Six days later, Mr Pelhousielie of Kohima was captured by Indian soldiers. 'Without killing him, they cut open his abdomen and scooped out his viscerals; thus their prisoner was able to die slowly in tormenting agony.'[61]

On the same day, army officers billeted in the Kohima High School kidnapped two young girls, Pfuzhunuo, aged 13, and Khunuo, aged 14. They were gang-raped by the regiment for hours, with all the officers venting their lust on the young Naga girls' bodies.

The Naga journalist and historian Kaka Iralu sums up this black period of his people's history:

> In the subsequent orgy of violence that engulfed these beautiful mountains and hills, a hundred thousand cries of agony rent the air and reverberated across the valleys and mountains of Nagaland, but their cries were never heard except by their tormentors. They bled, they cried and they died but the world never heard their cries of agony. Every Naga soul felt the repercussions of this nightmare. Every Naga family was desecrated and almost every village of every tribe was burned to ashes.[62]

7

Mayangkokla, a Sister in Christ

If one part suffers, every part suffers with it. . . .
Now you are the body of Christ, and each one of
you is a part of it.

1 Corinthians 12:26–27

February 27, 1957 dawned a cold day in the village of Ungma in the Naga Hills. A beautiful young Naga woman named Mayangkokla woke up early, wrapping herself in her traditional red-and-black shawl to keep out the winter chill. She was renowned for her innocence and her striking appearance. Taller than most Naga women, she had beautiful, clear skin and a sweetness that for many young single men in the surrounding villages made her the wife of their dreams.

Mayangkokla had two older brothers, Kikamongba and Markaba. That morning, the three of them had been assigned by the Naga army to help build a camp in a secret location in the mountains. At 6.30, they walked out of their village, eager to give their labour for the brave soldiers who were holding out against the Indian forces. Almost immediately, the three youngsters were surrounded by a contingent of the Jat Regiment, under the command of Major Trilok Singh. The Indian troops did not even bother to interrogate them, but started to kick and beat them with their rifle butts without mercy. After 15 minutes of this savage treatment, their clothes were torn and their bodies bloody.

The three Nagas were then marched a hundred yards or so to the church. On the way, one of the soldiers started to molest Mayangkokla. Kaka Iralu, who interviewed her long after these events, recounts what happened next:

Everywhere frightened villagers scattered in all directions as the procession wound its way toward the church. When they reached the church compound, Mayangkokla was stripped completely naked and in full view of the remaining villagers the soldiers raped her one after the other. The orgy would continue for at least an hour as the soldiers vented their lust on her beautiful body. The villagers could not bring themselves to watch this sadistic sight and turned their heads away. They were all seized with terrible anger but none could do anything as all the soldiers were armed to the teeth and cocked guns were pointed in their direction.

For Mayangkokla, this was a nightmare she could not believe was really happening. It was a desecration of her womanhood—a violation of her very humanity. Her screams of pain and cries for help were finally answered when an old woman, unable to bear the sight any more, came running out from a house with a cloth to cover her nakedness. She pleaded and cried, 'Please, no more. You have done enough.' As she tried to push her way into the circle of soldiers she was met with a battery of blows from rifle butts and barrels. There were still some soldiers who had not taken their turn. As they floored the old woman, [who fell] unconscious on the ground, bleeding profusely, they continued their orgy.

Both Kikamongba and Markaba were standing near the scene under guard. They had turned their heads away and both were crying, unable to do anything to save their sister.

When the soldiers were finished, both Kikamongba and the almost unconscious Mayangkokla were dragged inside the church. Kikamongba was ordered to remove his torn clothes. He fearfully obeyed. They were then ordered to commit sexual intercourse on the floor of the church. However frightened they were, both of them refused to comply with this. They pleaded, 'Please don't make us do that. This is the house of God, and we would be committing an unpardonable sin if we do this inside the church.' [In response] to this plea, the officer shouted an order and several soldiers came back with the fencing posts of the church. Their already lacerated bodies received another rain of blows from the heavy posts. The pain was so unbearable that they finally obeyed. As they were lying together thus, the soldiers formed a circle around them and laughed. Some of them clapped, while others shouted 'chabash' (well done).

Next, all three of them were tightly bound by ropes and blindfolded and taken to an army camp. When their blindfolds were removed, they found themselves inside some cells. It was only here that the interrogations began. They were very badly beaten again as unintelligible questions were asked of them. When nightfall came, some of the soldiers came in and dragged Mayangkokla from the cell. Pinning her against the walls and on the floor, [they raped her] repeatedly. In the one week that they were kept inside the army outpost, this sadistic ritual was repeated again and again and yet again.

By the third day, Markaba, the oldest among them, had gone insane. He began to scream and shout like a wild animal penned inside a cage. Even after they were released, Markaba never recovered his sanity. He died a madman.[63]

Forty-one years after these demonically-inspired events, Iralu met Mayangkokla at her village. As he held her hand and offered words of comfort, tears welled up in her eyes and she said,

Son, it has now been more than forty years, and in all these years no one has come to me with such words of sympathy. All the years I have borne the burden of that nightmare experience all alone. I see them in my dreams and wake up screaming. I see them even when I am awake. . . . Now I can die in peace, for you have taken it away from my mind. Tell it, my son; tell it to the world so that the pain and the humiliation that we have suffered for our nation will not be in vain.[64]

Mayangkokla died on October 23, 1998, nine months after she was finally allowed to tell her story to the world.

I have not included this account of what happened to her to be salacious but simply to show what just one young Naga was forced to suffer. When one talks of hundreds of villages burned and hundreds of thousands of people killed, it is easy to forget that these horrible statistics refer to real human beings like Mayangkokla and her brothers. They are all individuals precious to their loving heavenly Father, whose anger will one day burn against all the ungodly and those who refuse to love the truth.

Christian, one day in heaven I am sure you will meet Mayangkokla, and the thousands of young Naga women like her who suffered unmentionable abuses. But in that blessed place they will not bear the physical and emotional scars of their torment any longer—they will be whole, full of joy and safe in the arms of their loving Saviour.

> *They will be his people, and God himself will be with them and be their God. He will wipe every tear from their eyes. There will be no more death or mourning or crying or pain, for the old order of things has passed away.*
>   Revelation 21:3–4).

It would be bad enough if what happened to Mayangkokla was an isolated incident, but similar cruelties were suffered by thousands of Naga women and girls, some younger than 10 years of age—such as the mass rape of the women of the Yankeli Baptist Church, or the 24 female victims in the village of Chesiezouma. The list goes on and on.

When I first travelled to Nagaland, I asked one Baptist pastor what had been the most difficult thing that faced the Naga church during the years of revival. It should be no surprise that he replied, 'The most difficult thing we have had to do is to forgive.'

Let me conclude this chapter with a poem written by a friend of a young Naga woman named Rose, who committed suicide after being raped by several Indian soldiers at Oinam in July 1987. She was a beautiful 18-year-old, engaged to be married to a young man in her village, but after her ordeal she killed herself because she could not bear to live with the memory of her humiliation and shame.

Before Suicide

Let the dark day go from my mind
And let the day that I was born
Be blotted from memory
To save me from being left forlorn.

My soul, my body lies in shreds,
My faith in mankind all betrayed.
I cry to heaven for justice
For nowhere else can it be done
And I denounce those lustful brutes
Before the great celestial throne.

Dear one, grieve not for what I've done
For it is to Jehovah's breast
That I now go to wait for you,
Where all the weary are at rest.

8

The Nagas Fight Back

It is true that much of our Christian theology is formed by our experiences in life. For many Christians who live in the Western world, where comfort is pursued at all costs and persecution is something we only read about, that happens to believers in faraway places like China and North Korea, it is easy to say that all fighting is wrong. In some circles it is accepted without question that those who confess to be followers of Christ should never, under any circumstances, take up arms against their fellow human beings.

The issue of whether Christians should go to war has been debated by believers for centuries. Books have been written by godly men on both sides of the argument. It is not my intention to reopen the discussion here, but simply to state that we should be slow to judge from the comfort of our armchairs when we have never been in the position the Nagas found themselves in.

It should be pointed out that Naga Christians were often specifically targeted by Indian soldiers because of their faith. Christianity was—and still is—hated by many Indian people who view it as a foreign religion used by the British colonialists to seduce them and take over their land. The fact that many Nagas had converted to Christianity prior to the beginning of the fighting was seen by the Indians as one of the principal reasons they were so zealous in their pursuit of independence.

The last Governor-General of India, Chakravati Rajagopalachari, had told a Naga delegation on November 28, 1946: 'Nagas are at full liberty to do as they like, either to become part of India or to be separated if that were in their best interests.' In the same speech, however, he also stated:

> The government of India suspects [that] the foreign missionaries are inciting the people and hence all the foreign missionaries are ordered to leave Nagaland. All the responsibilities of the Naga Church should be left in the hands of the local church leaders.

To this day, many in India believe that the root cause of the numerous armed uprisings in north-east India was the influence of Christianity on the people there.

The Nagas, many of whom were active, Bible-believing Christians, were faced with two alternatives. Either they could kneel down and await not just certain death but the complete obliteration of their people or they could take up arms in self-defence. Other options, such as fleeing from Nagaland, were not considered. As one Naga historian notes,

> The question of surrender or retreat or migration to another country did not arise, simply because they had no other land on the whole face of this planet Earth besides Nagaland. To retreat or run away from their land and occupy another land would be to claim other people's land as their own. Hence the Nagas had no alternative but to stand and fight even if to do so meant sure death. . . . As far as the Nagas were concerned, the defence of their motherland was a moral and political duty. They owed it to themselves and their children and all future generations of Nagas to defend their God-apportioned land with all their strength and might.[65]

With few weapons and little organization, the various tribes joined together to fight against the Indian armies that had come to slaughter them. The greatest advantages they had were their knowledge of the terrain and their incredible ability to endure hardship in the jungles and mountains.

Multitudes of Nagas went on the move, as entire villages and clans abandoned their homes and hid from death in the remote hills. These proved far from safe, however, as the Indian Air Force was mobilized to bomb the refugees from the air. The Naga soldiers could not win a conventional war against the huge Indian forces, so they resorted to guerrilla tactics to gain an edge over their better-armed enemy. Ambush became a favourite technique.

For many hundreds of thousands of Nagas, starvation became a real threat as the war raged on. The Indian Army customarily burned and destroyed fields, livestock and granaries as it raped its way across Nagaland. For two years, no crops were planted as the people hid in the hills, surviving on roots and the bark of trees and the occasional small animal or bird they managed to catch. The weakest elements of their society—the elderly and the small children—fared the worst. Countless thousands perished.

The Bible became very real and precious to many of the Christians during these extreme hardships. Often heads were bowed as fervent prayers and petitions went up to heaven from the peaks of the Naga Hills, as people called on the name of the Lord Jesus Christ to save them.

After all the foreign missionaries had been expelled from Nagaland in the early 1950s, the Naga church found itself without adequate leadership. The missionaries had done many great things over the years, but they had failed to anticipate the sudden change that would sweep over the country and consequently had failed to train enough local pastors to lead the church when they were gone. Now, all external support was removed. All of a sudden there were no churches to worship in, no chapels for prayer meetings and few clergy to minister the word of God.

Instead of a building in which to perform religious duties, the Naga Christians came to see that the Church was them, a living, breathing organ—the Body of Christ. They no longer needed four walls within which to express their faith. They simply needed the person and power of Jesus Christ. Instead of relying

on ordained ministers for their spiritual sustenance, they were
obliged to depend on the Holy Spirit for comfort and guidance.
One historian notes: 'This became a blessing in disguise. . . .
They took it as a challenge and assumed the full responsibility.
. . . Unprecedented energy and enthusiasm were found in them.'[66]
Prayer meetings were held wherever two or more believers were
gathered—in the jungle, on the mountain trails or in the torture
chamber of the prison.

Many Christians may struggle to understand how such a
diabolical war, which resulted in the deaths of at least 200,000
Nagas, could coincide with one of the mightiest spiritual revivals
in the Church's history—and yet it did. As Hevukhu Achumi
Sema later reflected:

> The political unrest brought untold misery and suffering
> upon all the citizens of Nagaland. Very often the human
> suffering and misery led people to seek God. Many fell
> away, but others kept their faith and started praying with
> tears . . . Many realized that the need of the hour was
> revival. There was a spiritual hunger for God in the hearts
> of many Christians and churches in Nagaland.[67]

9

The Fiery Furnace

If we are thrown into the blazing furnace, the
God we serve is able to save us from it, and he
will rescue us from your hand, O king. But even if
he does not, we want you to know, O king, that we
will not serve your gods.

Daniel 3:17–18

In this text, three young Jewish men refused to compromise their faith in the one true God, even if it should cost them their lives. In the event, they were miraculously saved from the fiery furnace of the Babylonian king. Just why God on some occasions chooses to move sovereignly to protect his followers from evil and on other occasions looks on silently as evil appears to triumph is a mystery known only by him.

In later chapters, you will read remarkable firsthand accounts of how God did help the Naga Christians, often with supernatural miracles that left their persecutors dumbfounded. But the following story also needs to be told. Unlike Daniel's friends (and Daniel himself), these three Naga men experienced indescribable hardship with no sign of a miraculous escape. It is not a pretty story, but neither does the Bible gloss over the tragedies and horrors of life, but simply records things as they happened.

* * * * * *

In 1961, while on a mission to obtain food for their battalion, three Naga soldiers were ambushed by Indian troops at a place called Pedihuru. The first of the trio was Sergeant Tsorelie from the village of Mezoma. He had grown up as the eldest of five children and as such had assumed more responsibility than most other boys his age. This habit of leadership contributed to a rapid rise through the ranks after he joined the Naga army in 1956. The other men captured were Sergeant Yanipra and Lieutenant Lhoulhe.

At gunpoint, the three men were taken to the Indian brigade headquarters at Piphema. This place had a horrible reputation among the Nagas. Many who entered it were never seen again. It was rumoured that the walls of the torture chambers were coated with a thick layer of dried human blood. Men were often hung upside-down by their ankles and tortured with a variety of instruments until they choked on their own blood and died. The three men had also heard stories of naked prisoners being electrocuted until their minds and bodies could no longer handle the pain and their heads literally exploded onto the ceiling and walls of the torture chamber.

Knowing they faced the same fate as many of their compatriots before them, the three men, all fine physical specimens in the prime of life, quietly yet defiantly made a covenant with each other that they would never divulge any details of their battalion's location and would never give their persecutors the satisfaction of hearing them scream or beg for mercy.

Prepared for the worst, Tsorielie, Yanipra and Lhoulhe were shocked when they were treated quite well for the first four days. They were locked up in separate cells and were given food that was the best they had tasted for some time. Such tactics were often employed by the Indians as a way to psychologically disarm new prisoners, who often entered the camp with stubborn minds. They also fed their prisoners well so that they would be able to survive the terrible interrogation for longer and would therefore (the Indians hoped) reveal more than they might have done if they had been subjected to it in an already weakened condition.

On the fifth morning of their captivity, their treatment abruptly changed. The three men were dragged from their cells, stripped naked and put in a large, windowless room. Immediately, before a word had been spoken, a storm of blows rained down upon them, knocking out teeth and scarring faces. The leaders of the interrogation were a Major Rai and a captain of the Garhwal Regiment. They spoke through Naga translators who hid their shame behind black cloths to conceal their identity.

Over the next few days, countless questions were asked of Tsorielie, Yanipra and Lhoulhe, mostly to do with troop locations, military strategy and supply routes. The three men did not know most of the answers, but anyway would never have betrayed their friends and fellow soldiers. Each refusal to talk was met with a flurry of blows. They were hung upside-down and occasionally subjected to electric shocks. At other times, huge wooden logs were rolled over their naked bodies. But, despite the excruciating pain, these brave men never screamed out or begged for relief, though they could not prevent the involuntary groans that came out as their ribs were fractured and their swollen bodies suffered brutal abuse.

On the fourth day, a heinous new form of torture was inflicted on them. The forests of Nagaland contain perhaps the world's hottest chilli peppers, known as Raja Mircha ('King Chilli') to locals, who use it sparingly in their dishes because of its potency. Just a tiny smear on the skin can cause a burning sensation for hours unless it is washed off with soap and water.

Tsorielie, Yanipra and Lhoulhe shook with horror as a whole plate of Raja Mircha was brought into the interrogation room. The torturers sneezed and their eyes watered as, slowly and deliberately, they crushed the chillies into a paste. Then, having bound the hands of the Nagas tightly behind their backs, they proceeded to inflict the most dreadful torment on these defenceless men, smearing the paste on their genitals and even pulling back their foreskins to apply it.

Despite the covenant the three had made before their tortures commenced, this cruelty was too much for them to endure. They howled like crazed animals as the chilli burned into their most delicate parts. Within minutes, their genitals had swollen to the thickness of their wrists. Their haunted screams were so loud that even people walking in the village below the camp could hear them.

Somehow, by God's grace, Yanipra and Lhoulhe were able to survive the torture. Over the coming weeks and months in prison, their bodies and minds slowly healed. Tsorielie, however, never recovered from the horrific ordeal. The next day, his two fellow prisoners noticed that he had started mumbling to himself. By the time his brother Kou was allowed into the camp to visit him a week later, he was already insane. His face was still swollen and covered with welts, bruises and blood, his body and mind destroyed. This firebrand soldier, who as a youth had loved wrestling, who had been noted for his manliness and courage, had been reduced to a broken shell.

Tsorielie was taken away from Nagaland to serve a term in the Tezpur Jail in the neighbouring state of Assam. None of his family was told where he had been moved to and it took them six months to track him down. Selling all he had, Kou secured what he believed to be his brother's release, but it turned out to be nothing more than a transfer. Tsorielie was moved to the Dimapur Central Jail, where he was incarcerated for another three years. He was finally released on September 6, 1964.

He made his way back to his home village, where in his confused state of mind he insisted on reporting for duty to his battalion headquarters. He built himself a hut in the jungle and lived there for the next 30 years, fishing and hunting, and returning to the village only when his rice rations ran out. In 1995, he moved to the town, saying that he was now too old to live in the jungle.

In 1998, Tsorielie was interviewed by Kaka Iralu, the Naga journalist who has documented many of the atrocities of the India–Naga War. Now 37 years after his excruciating experience

at Piphema, he had never recovered his mind, but his will had not
been broken. Iralu summarizes the conversation:

> I expressed my appreciation for his long service as a Naga
> soldier and also my respect for his uncompromising
> stand. 'Yes, my son, it has been very long, the struggle
> has lasted for so many years, but we shall never give
> up.' . . . Shaking with anger, he said, '*Lasiezoto! Kilazoto!*
> *Khashulie Ihozo!*' ('We shall rise up again! We shall do
> battle again! We shall never give up!').
>
> I was deeply moved by that agitated reply. Here was a
> mad man stating the facts very clearly and swearing that
> he would never give up.[68]

10

Does Anyone Care?

Revivals are dangerous. They are fatal to the kingdom of darkness. They are like a temporary transfer of humanity to heaven; a transient glimpse of what it is like living in the manifest glory of God.

Winkie Pratney

The years of death and destruction among the Nagas left them disillusioned and disheartened. It seemed as if the world had abandoned them to suffer and die in isolation. Yet it was at the lowest point of their despair that revival broke out among the Nagas—surely one of the most powerful and far-reaching revivals ever to have impacted a people at any time in history. For indeed there had been one Witness who had seen the suffering of the Nagas, One who cared for them and longed to show his love and compassion to them: the Lord Jesus Christ. Even during the savage Indian attacks, God had not allowed evil to have a completely free reign.

He humbled you, causing you to hunger and then feeding you with manna, which neither you nor your fathers had known, to teach you that man does not live on bread alone but on every word that comes from the mouth of the Lord.
Deuteronomy 8:3

In some places, such as the village of Sendenyu near Tseminyu, God sovereignly took care of his people. The believers there asked the Lord to provide their daily bread, according to his word, and he mercifully answered their prayers by providing them with a form of manna, just as he had provided for the hungry Children of Israel as they wandered in the desert many centuries before. In this case it was a wild creeper, known locally as kenrhü, which had large, edible roots that tasted like potato. Every family in Sendenyu collected just what they needed for that day. If anyone collected the 'manna' for the next day they would not be able to eat it, because it starts to stink and taste bitter if left overnight. This food was eaten by the villagers for every meal for almost a year, until they were able to plant some of their crops again.

> 'No weapon forged against you will prevail. . . . This is
> the heritage of the servants of the Lord, and this is their
> vindication from me,' declares the Lord.
>
> Isaiah 54:17

One evening in 1959, while an evening worship service was in progress at the Sendenyu Baptist Church, soldiers of the Indian 7th Gorkha Regiment came and surrounded the building. Inspired by the hosts of hell, they decided to massacre the entire congregation. Without warning, they opened fire for several minutes, spraying hundreds of bullets into the thatch roof and walls. They riddled the building with holes, but when they looked inside they were amazed to find that none of the believers was harmed. Not one hair on their heads had been hurt. Confused, but determined to do the job, the soldiers then lobbed three hand grenades into the church. When the Christians saw them roll across the floor they immediately dropped to their knees, covered the grenades with their hands and cried out to God for his protection. None of the weapons exploded.

Finally, the Indian commander ordered his men to use machine-guns to annihilate the congregation. Astonishingly, all of the bullets discharged through the chambers somehow failed to hurt any of the believers. The soldiers, now afraid and aware that God's hand was against them, hurriedly withdrew back to their base, leaving the Christians alone.

An interesting footnote to this testimony is that during the attempted massacre the troops had also fired their rifles indiscriminately amongst the houses of the village. That night, there were four Christians who happened to have stayed at home instead of going to the service: Vilhoulie Kent, Yhunlonyu Kent, Alisa Kemp and Tenuyhun Seb. All four were hit by bullets, which pierced their clothes and left unmistakable holes in them—but then fell to the ground without penetrating their skin. None of them was harmed or injured in any way.

For everyone who asks receives; he who seeks finds; and to him who knocks, the door will be opened.

Luke 11:10

One way the Lord Jesus Christ showed his loving concern for the plight of the Nagas during their years of turmoil is illustrated in the following stories.

When a boy called Nichulo Rengma of the village of Nyishunyu saw the dead and mutilated body of his father, he was shocked and traumatized. Without saying a word, he picked up a gun and went into the forest. When he did not return, the villagers organized search parties, but after three days there was still no sign of the boy. Seven days after his disappearance, a message was sent to the Sendenyu Baptist Church asking the believers there to pray for the missing child.

As they did so, the Holy Spirit gave them a vision, in which they saw the lost boy sitting under a big, brown tree in the forest, east of the timber mill in the Nyishunyu area. A message was sent to his relatives and they immediately went to this particular tree and found him sitting there, exactly as the Lord had revealed. The village of Sendenyu is a long way from Nyishunyu, so the Christians there had absolutely no knowledge of the place where the boy was found.

> *Suddenly an angel of the Lord appeared and a light shone*
> *in the cell. . . . 'Quick, get up!' he said, and the chains fell*
> *off Peter's wrists.*
>
> Acts 12:7

In May 1962, Ngaseng Kent and Solomon Kent were arrested by the Rajput Regiment of the Indian Army and were handed over to the 11th Gorkha Regiment for interrogation. They were bound together with iron chains and delivered to the military barracks at a place called Zubza.

The two prisoners prayed continually for God's protection and help, but despite their prayers their situation seemed only to get worse and the order was given that they should be shot. While they waited for the executioner to arrive, these men committed their souls to the Lord's care—and as they were doing so, the Holy Spirit revealed to Solomon Kent that he should not be afraid because the Lord was with him in his trial. The executioner came and took aim at the first of them. They closed their eyes and waited for the bullet that would send them into eternity with their loving Saviour.

After a few seconds, they opened their eyes again and saw that the rifle had failed to go off. One of the Indian officers, a second lieutenant, became outraged at the weapon's failure. He checked the rifle and the bullets and then, intensely angry, he went to beat the two defenceless men with the butt—but as he raised the rifle above his head, it stuck in a rope that was holding the tent and he struck himself on the forehead. At this, he threw the gun down and began to weep, seemingly aware that a greater power was against him and his evil plan.

The prisoners were sent back to their cell, as those in charge considered what action to take against them. After a while, Ngaseng Kent dozed off and had a dream in which the Lord revealed that the believers at Sendenyu were praying earnestly for him and he should get up and escape immediately. He woke up and when he touched the iron chains that shackled him, they suddenly broke off, setting him free.

Ngaseng told his astonished friend what God had shown him in his dream. He prayed for Solomon, but his chains did not break. The two men decided that Ngaseng ought to obey God, so he made his escape. The guards gave chase but they could not catch him.

This was not the first time that a Christian had experienced such a miraculous deliverance. In 1957, Kesinga Seb was arrested and taken to the jungle. When he asked the Lord of Lords for help, the chains that bound him loosened by themselves, allowing him to run off. The Indian soldiers shot at him and threw grenades at him, but the Living God granted his prayer and he escaped unharmed.

When you walk through the fire, you will not be burned; the flames will not set you ablaze. For I am the Lord, your God, the Holy One of Israel, your Saviour.

Isaiah 43:2–3

An elderly farmer, Kesinlo Seb, lived on the banks of the large, beautiful Lake Ndayhun Zi, where he had a terraced field and a fruit farm. He also caught fish in the lake, and picked local medicinal herbs which the people of the surrounding villages used to cure colds and other ailments. In order to worship the Lord and enjoy fellowship, he walked to the nearest village every Saturday night, stayed for the Sunday services and then returned home on Monday.

During the war with India, a squad of soldiers happened to pass by his farmhouse. They beat the old man black and blue, and then their commander ordered them to burn him alive. They bound his hands and feet and prepared a large fire, and then two men took hold of him, one by the legs, the other by the arms, and threw him into the flames, to die a horrible death while everyone watched. But, strangely, Kesinlo Seb went right through the fire and landed on the other side. Not a single hair on his head was harmed. The two soldiers lost their balance as they threw him and stumbled into the flames themselves, suffering minor burns.

'My grace is sufficient for you, for my power is made perfect in weakness.'

2 Corinthians 12:9

In April 1959, a well-known Indian Army officer, a Major Thomas, decided to annihilate the people of Sendenyu. This village had provoked the wrath of the Indians because it was one of the first to hoist the flag of the Independent Republic of Nagaland and the villagers were known to be actively helping the Naga soldiers hiding out in the mountains.

Two days before the arrival of Major Thomas and his men, the people of Sendenyu were alerted to his plans to massacre them and reduce their village to ashes. Trembling, they gathered in the church and prayed to the Merciful God for deliverance from the cruel hand of the devil. The Holy Spirit spoke through various people and instructed the villagers how to receive the Indian officer. The Lord told them not to be afraid, because he was with them. They were to welcome Major Thomas at the village gate, on the eastern side, singing the hymn 'Let Him In'.

To continue the story in the words of eyewitnesses:

> They were to stand in a row, with the Pastor in the front, followed by the little children, then the young girls and women folks and so on. Upon his arrival, everyone should greet him by the way of shaking hands with him, all the while singing the proposed hymn as they escorted him to the church. It was further instructed that once they reached the doorstep of the church, the Major's shoes should be removed and his feet washed. Then he must be made to sit at the pulpit next to the Pastor, and time allotted for him to give a speech. . . .

Before reaching the village, the Major and his troops came burning the shacks in the fields that lay on his way. This terrified the villagers, but the Lord God, through the power of the Holy Spirit, reminded them not to be afraid because he was with them.

Upon his arrival at the reception gate at the village entrance, the Pastor, children and everyone in the row greeted him by shaking his hands, singing songs, and escorted him to the church.

At the church entrance, the believers took off the Major's shoes, washed his feet and made him sit with the Pastor at the pulpit. The congregation prayed for him and gave him time to deliver a speech to them.

Major Thomas then stood up in the pulpit and started trembling. His voice stammering, he said that he had been sent by the Government of India to destroy the village of Sendenyu. 'I, therefore, have come to burn down Sendenyu village to ashes and wipe out the people in it.'

The Major continued, saying that his intentions had completely changed at the village gate when he saw the little children singing joyful songs.

Before parting the next day, Major Thomas told the villagers that he would supply rice to them [because he had destroyed their fields] as soon as he reached his station at Chiechama village, until the time of the next harvest. And true to his promise, he supplied rice to the village of Sendenyu till harvest that year.

Major Thomas also instructed the military truck drivers to give a lift to any citizens of Sendenyu on their way between Kohima and Tseminyu. As long as Major Thomas was posted at Chiechama, he helped the people of Sendenyu.[69]

11

The 1950s: A Cry for Mercy

Amidst the extreme hardship imposed by the war with India, the hapless Nagas called out for God's mercy. Heaven answered in the 1950s by sending the first rolling waves of what was to be one of the most powerful and comprehensive revivals in Christian history. To the natural mind, the church in Nagaland looked anything but ready for an awakening. All the missionaries had been expelled from the region, leaving many believers feeling orphaned by their sudden departure. War had decimated Naga communities and left multitudes of people destitute.

The presence and transforming power of the Holy Spirit started to work tribe by tribe, village by village and house by house. One Christian leader said,

> When the missionaries were kicked out, we didn't know what to do! We were so desperate that all we could think of doing was seeking the Lord. We fell on our faces and cried out to him for his help. When God responded with power from heaven, the revival swept from home to home, with simple farmers and mothers telling the gospel to other simple farmers and mothers. In this way the fire swept thousands of people into the Kingdom of God.[70]

The coming of the revival was a surprise to most people, but some had been praying for a visitation of God for years. The missionary Dr G E Hunteri, who worked among the Ao, was described as

> . . . a man of God, praying, preaching and practising holy living. He was ordered to leave the Naga Hills in 1952. He had a heavy burden for revival among the Nagas. On the morning of the day he departed, he was praying for

hours in his bathroom, praying in agony that God might visit the Nagas with an outpouring of the Holy Spirit. The answer of Hunteri's prayers was the awakening which soon began in 1952 under the leadership of Rev. Rikum, a personal associate of Hunteri. Christians were praying in tears, confessions were made and so many experienced the visitation of the Holy Spirit. . . . Prayer meetings and Christian fellowship became life-forces. The awakening vitalized the youth and women['s] organizations. Evangelistic enterprises were further intensified, and outreach missions were set up.[71]

In the early days, the evangelists Imkong Toshi and Neihulie Angami and a few others travelled to different tribes and held meetings. Revival broke out in many churches. Christians sought God's face in humility and deep prayer. Some church leaders, however, hesitated to accept the revival as a move of God and they organized a rally to question Toshi and Angami. Some local believers were fasting and praying that same day and while the two evangelists were speaking, a local Christian stood up and stated:

> Friends, since these preachers have come, many people are turning to Christ, with broken hearts, confessing their sins to God in repentance. Every day many sick people are coming to them for prayer. I never knew that there were so many sinners and sick people in this town until these preachers came.[72]

In 1952, at Longkhum in Mokokchung District, some of the Naga believers were gathered together at midday when suddenly a rainbow appeared in the sky, even though it was a bright, sunny day. As they pondered this mystery, they all heard a loud, clear voice saying, 'This revival will be spread all over Nagaland.'[73]

During the Sumi Baptist Bible Conference in Sukhalu from March 11 to 15, 1954, 'all the delegates felt the presence of

God and were touched by the Holy Spirit as they experienced revival for the first time.'[74] The weather at this time of the year was extremely hot, windy and dusty, so that few people attended the meetings. The church leaders prayed and shed tears before the Lord, beseeching him to send rain and God answered their prayers. Rain immediately began to fall. The weather became much more pleasant and people flocked to the meetings.

God's mighty power also touched the Zeliangrong Nagas at this time. One pastor recalls:

> I immediately knew that I was in the presence of the Almighty God. Anyone who has truly had this kind of experience will not doubt the reality of God or the truth that all power and authority in heaven and on the earth have been given to Jesus Christ. The Holy Spirit revealed my sins at this meeting and with a feeling of terrible dread and shame I confessed all my sins to him. It was like a great weight was released from my back and immediately I was filled with overwhelming joy.[75]

Throughout the 1950s the revival continued to be marked by deep repentance of sin, coupled with numerous instances of miraculous intervention.

> Many miracles of healing were witnessed. Blind eyes were opened, deaf ears were healed, crippled bodies were restored and even the dead were raised. In one village a woman was dead for about four hours, her loved ones and neighbours were crying and weeping for her; Evangelist Zhowheyi went and prayed for her at midnight and she came back to life. God is still performing miracles.[76]

Before the revival, the Baptist churches had been very formal, controlled by a hierarchy of church leaders. Meetings were structured and little or no emotion was ever displayed by believers. When the Holy Spirit started to move in great power, the man-made structures of control were swept away. As in the Book of

Acts, spontaneous prayer and evangelism took place everywhere as people celebrated the new life they had experienced in Jesus Christ.

> Even the form of worship and the conventional method of praying, singing and preaching were changed. Meetings went unplanned, and informal. Prayer meetings continued for hours. Very often preachers stopped their preaching in the middle of their sermon because people in the congregation would cry out for mercy. Many times people would stand up under heavy burden of sin and confess their sins before God and even before the congregation.[77]

A great awakening blossomed among the Lotha in the 1950s. The power of God shook their communities to their foundations, and numerous miracles and 'signs and wonders' occurred which put the fear of God into all the people. A strange incident took place in 1954 in the village of Phiro in Wokha District:

> While the believers were gathered together praying, the church was lifted up from the ground about two to three feet. Even unbelievers saw this miracle and many repented from their sins. But in this village, although the majority became Christians, there was a remnant that refused to change and they swore to each other that they would never become Christians. One night these hardened unbelievers were merrymaking in a house when the devil himself manifested in their midst, scaring them so much that they ran straight to the church and repented, throwing off their foolish vow.[78]

On September 22, 1957, some believers in the town of Wokha were gathered together for prayer when suddenly tongues of fire could be seen flickering just above the roof of the church building. People from all over the town rushed to see this miracle and were amazed. Numerous eyewitnesses to this event still live in Wokha today.

After the Holy Spirit swept down from heaven, all the gifts of the Spirit as listed in the Bible were experienced in the Naga churches. 'Blind eyes were opened, deaf and dumb were healed, the sick and demon-possessed were healed.... Out of all miracles, salvation of a sinner is the greatest miracle.'[79]

Pastor Zhowhuyi of the village of Chesezu recalls the state of the church in those days:

> The gospel of Jesus Christ had arrived among my tribe—the Chakhesang—many years before Jesus himself came and visited us in great revival power!

> Christianity was respected by many Chakhesang people prior to the revival, but few really knew what it meant to walk with Jesus and to love God with all their hearts, minds and souls. Our church services were very low-key and conservative, and there was little fire or life to be found in most believers. As a result, few people were attracted to the message of the gospel, as they saw the Christians' lives were little different from the lives of unbelievers. The only visible difference was the Christians went to a building every Sunday where they participated in strange religious duties.[80]

In the village of Khulazu Basa in 1958–59, during the height of the revival, people were so busy seeking the Lord that they had no time to plant or take care of their crops. In an agricultural community the result should have been a disaster, but God intervened and miraculously huge pumpkins started to grow. Sometimes two or three large pumpkins grew from a single branch. In consequence, the people did not starve and they continued to serve the Lord with great joy.[81]

Not only were the gifts of the Spirit fully in evidence among the Nagas, but they were matched by the fruit of the Spirit that was produced in the lives of the believers. The church that had become lukewarm and worldly during the years of the Second World War was now on fire for God! A great change came over the people and the moral climate of the society was totally transformed. Neihulie Angami recalls:

> The fruit of the Holy Spirit, 'love, joy, peace, long-suffering, kindness, goodness, faith, meekness, and temperance', could all be seen in the daily life of the believers. The heathen saw the wonderful change that had come over the Christians and it simply overwhelmed them. Believers sang songs of redemption in churches, in homes, in public buses, in farms and in woods. Christians in processions marched through the villages and towns singing songs and praising God. The Spirit of praise was seen all over, bringing peace to the troubled and weary, and joy to the sorrowful.[82]

12

One Church's Story

All the different tribes in Nagaland today have been deeply
affected by the light and power of the gospel. The miracles and
signs and wonders that accompanied the revival are so numerous
that it would take a book thousands of pages long just to begin
to record God's wonderful works. This chapter recounts some
of the remarkable testimonies about what happened in the
Sendenyu Baptist Church near Tseminyu.[83] The members of this
congregation are all from the smallest tribe in Nagaland, the
Rengma, which today numbers only about 22,000.

The people of Sendenyu were in a desperate state at the time
God sent revival to their midst. In 1955 and '56, they were forced
to flee for their lives into the surrounding mountains and jungles.
The Indian authorities lured many of them out with promises
of peace, but then rounded them up and herded them into the
prison camp at Tseminyu, where they were held for a year or
so. In consequence, no food was cultivated in the village for two
whole years.

> The people struggled to live on jungle roots and wild
> leaves until the harvest arrived. But even under such
> stark and harrowing conditions, the people did not turn
> to God for help . . . but continued to live sinful lives of
> hatred, strife, selfishness, envy, drunkenness, adultery,
> fornication, and every such thing that is a work of the
> flesh.[84]

The Sendenyu Baptist Church had existed for many years before
the events that shook the congregation in February 1959. The
faith and commitment of the believers had grown rather weak,

as many had lost their spiritual fervour and become apathetic; but in that month, by the grace of God, they started to become increasingly aware of their sins. Spontaneous confession began to break out in their meetings. After pouring out their souls and receiving God's forgiveness, they found that their sorrow was washed away by overflowing peace, joy and happiness.

One evening, after three consecutive nights of special meetings, most of the congregation started leaving the church to go to their homes. Some, however, stayed in the building and continued in prayer and worship, sensing that God wanted to do something new in their midst. Suddenly, a flame of fire appeared in the church in full view of many people. It came down and settled over the pulpit at the front of the sanctuary. The people were shocked and awestruck, as the fire was accompanied by a mighty sound like a loud roar. The flame divided into tongues of fire. Some people immediately began to prophesy, while others saw awesome visions.

This was the start of the tremendous visitation of the Holy Spirit among this body of believers. They came to despair over their hopeless state of rebellion and realized that their only hope was complete submission to the True and Living God. They also came to understand that their greatest acts of self-righteousness were no more than filthy rags in the sight of God. Only Jesus Christ and the word of God could satisfy the deep spiritual longings they all felt.

On one occasion, Pastor Kegwahi Kent was praying at midnight for the nations of the world. Suddenly the fire of the Lord descended on his home, illuminating the whole house. It settled on top of his head and burned all the way down to the tips of his toes, and he was overwhelmed by God's power and presence. All of a sudden, an angel appeared to him and commanded him to preach the gospel to every household. Pastor Kent felt completely inadequate to accomplish such a task, as he could not speak the languages and dialects of any of the other Naga tribes.

He was also told that all preachers should live according to the message they preached—their lives should not be inconsistent with their words. Singers, too, should live according to the message of their songs, and anyone who prayed should live according to their prayers.

Over the days and weeks that followed, many people stood up in the church and, under the power of the Holy Spirit, exposed the secret sins of other members of the congregation. Often, verses from the Bible were quoted accurately that expressly revealed the state of someone's heart in a way that only God could have known.

During one worship service, a member of the church prophesied that God would send a pillar of fire and that everyone must confess and repent of their sins. He also said that, when it came, the fire would burn down an unbeliever's house. The whole congregation gathered that evening and earnestly prayed and confessed their sins to the Lord. Suddenly, some time between 7 and 8 pm, a strange pillar of fire shone above the church. Its light was so pure that it was brighter than noontime on a sunny day, and it cast no shadow or reflection in any direction. It was unlike any other light the people had seen before.

After a short time, the pillar of fire vanished. The people then noticed that the house of a non-Christian named Tesinlo Khing was in flames! The fire raged out of control. In those days, there was hardly any gap between the houses in the village. Their walls were mats and their roofs were made of thatch and yet, as everyone observed, the destroying fire miraculously did not spread to any of the neighbouring houses, which were owned by Christians.

The Lord hurled large hailstones down on them from the sky.

Joshua 10:11

On another occasion at Sendenyu, Mrs Rosenle Seb brought a prophecy that if people continued to murmur against the workings of the Holy Spirit, hailstones would be poured down from heaven to undo their unbelief. No sooner had she finished speaking than a storm of hailstones came from the heavens, crashing down on the church roof in broad daylight, without a single drop of accompanying rain.

On yet another occasion, a similar message was given during a worship meeting, that because of people's murmurings and unbelief God was sending a shower of rain from heaven to undo their doubt. Immediately, a heavy shower enveloped the village, even though it was a completely cloudless day.

Through many such signs and wonders God showed 'the distinction between the righteous and the wicked, between those who serve God and those who do not' (Malachi 3:18). The fear of God fell on the entire village and many were added to the church.

Those whom I love I rebuke and discipline. So be earnest, and repent.

Revelation 3:19

During the revival, many people committed their lives to Christ, but some sinners resisted the conviction of the Holy Spirit. One such man was Gwanilo Seb, a notorious drunkard who had been excommunicated from the church because of his unrepentant heart. He was furious and was looking for a way to persecute and humiliate the believers he felt had rejected him.

One evening, although he did not believe that the revival was God-sent, Gwanilo and two of his friends came to the door of the church to satisfy their curiosity. An elderly Christian man, Jihlo Bukh, saw him standing by the door and took hold of his hands and pulled him towards the pulpit at the front of the sanctuary. Gwanilo started to tremble all over from the fear of God. All of a sudden, an invisible hand struck him so hard on the back of his head that he fell to the ground and couldn't speak.

For a whole day, as the conviction of the Holy Spirit broke down his stubborn heart, Gwanilo was dumb. Finally, he motioned for a piece of chalk and wrote on the church blackboard, asking the believers to forgive him and to pray for his readmission into the church. They duly prayed for him, but still he could not speak; but the instant they took out the church membership book and wrote his name in the register, he regained the power of speech. Gwanilo Seb became a committed and active member of the church.

As for Jihlo Bukh, who had taken him by the arm and pulled him into the church, God did an unusual miracle for him. He had never received a formal education and now that he was an old man he regretted that he had never learned to read the Bible or the hymn-book. During the revival he received a divine enablement from the Holy Spirit so that he was suddenly able to read fluently. This gift completely changed his life. He was so grateful to God that he read his word day and night.[85]

God continued to work powerfully in the hearts of the Rengma, purifying and empowering them for service. The fear of the Lord gripped the whole community. All that mattered to believers was obedience to his will. People desired the meat of God's word more than they desired their lunch and dinner.

Some of the miracles that took place in Nagaland were quite exceptional. At least four people were raised from the dead. These events were witnessed by hundreds of people, who have given firsthand testimonies about what they saw.

One day, Pastor Kegwahi Kent fired his gun, an old muzzle-loader such as is used by many people in Nagaland. On this occasion, the gun exploded near the firing pin, causing serious injury to its owner's face and hands. Over the days that followed, his condition grew worse until he fell into a coma and died. A doctor was summoned and he confirmed that the pastor's heart had stopped functioning and declared him dead.

In keeping with Naga tradition, the church bell was rung to inform the community of his tragic demise. Funeral arrangements were made. However, the believers who were attending to the corpse continued to pray, refusing to believe that their beloved pastor had so suddenly departed from this life. They pleaded with the Lord to bring him back. Many believed that his death was the result of a satanic attack, rather than the will of God wanting to take his servant home.

According to Kegwahi Kent himself, after he died he was approached by a man or an angel dressed in white, who told him not to worry, because God had ordained that he would be healed. As the man left, the pastor came back to life and regained consciousness. Over the weeks that followed, he gradually recovered from his injuries, and eventually he was able to return to the ministry of preaching God's word for many more years.

When you pass through the waters, I will be with you; and when you pass through the rivers, they will not sweep over you.

Isaiah 43:2

The monsoon season in Nagaland lasts from around April to November every year. During the rains, roads and trails turn into mud, landslides are common and rivers are impassable. On one occasion during the revival, the Lord told the prayer group at the Sendenyu Baptist Church that they must take the message of repentance and faith to surrounding communities and tribes. Through prophecy, the Holy Spirit told the believers the exact date and time they should cross the River Nra to share the gospel with various Sumi villages on the western side.

On the day ordained, the evangelistic team obeyed God's command and made its way towards the river. The Nra is the widest and deepest river in all the territory occupied by the Rengma and when they reached its bank they found it in full flood and impossible to cross. There were no bridges or boats to take them to the other side. Some of them wanted to turn back, but others remembered how the Lord had spoken to them and commanded them to go that day. The group decided that they must obey God's command at all costs. They prayed and asked the Lord to protect them from the raging waters and enable them to witness for his glory.

Then the faithful believers took a step into the river—and then another, then yet another. They were surprised to find that the water was not as deep as they had thought. So, they boldly walked across to the other side, and as they crossed, they said, they could feel the bed of the river under the soles of their bare feet. To this day, they are not sure how God enabled them to cross the Nra— they seem to think the Lord somehow made the river shallow for a while. At the place in question, the water was later measured and found to be at least 30 feet deep during the rainy season.

These miracles all took place in and around a single village, but they are typical of thousands of similar events that occurred throughout the length and breadth of Nagaland during the revival years. According to one account from Sendenyu,

> Peace and tranquility and health, economic progress and prosperity prevailed in the village. Disputes, quarrelling and social disorders were hardly heard of or seen or experienced during the first seven years of revival in Sendenyu.[86]

However, one sad observation about every genuine revival throughout history is that in the end the sinful nature of men and women invariably finds a way to frustrate the workings of the Holy Spirit and the revival fires die down. So it was in Sendenyu. The people had firsthand experience of the life and power of God, but according to their church's own souvenir booklet, published in 1984,

> From 1967 onwards, the believers began to turn backward to their former state of sinful life again, as 'the dog is turned to his own vomit again, and the sow that was washed to her wallowing in the mire' (2 Peter 2:22

[KJV]). They backslid, and turned their backs on the Lord their God, and paid their attention to worldly affairs, leaving their first love.[87]

13

Opposition Stiffens

Slandering revivals will often put them down. The
great revival in the days of President Edwards suffered
greatly by the conduct of the Church in this respect. It
is to be expected that the enemies of God will revile,
misrepresent, and slander revivals. But when the
Church herself engages in this work, and many of her
most influential members are aiding and abetting in
calumniating and misrepresenting a glorious work of
God, it is reasonable that the Spirit should be grieved
away. It cannot be denied that this has been done to a
grievous and God-dishonouring extent.

Charles Finney, 1837

Every true revival in church history has experienced great
opposition. Satan cannot stand to see God's unbridled power on
the loose, changing and restoring thousands of lives—'plundering
hell to populate heaven', as one modern-day evangelist has
described it. There have always been two main kinds of opposition
to revival. The first occurs when unbelievers rise up and try to stop
a move of God. It could be said that the Apostle Paul's preaching
resulted in one of two things: revival or riot—and sometimes
both! This kind of opposition, from those who do not know the
truth, is to be expected.

A far more insidious opposition, however, is that which comes
from within the Body of Christ. All through Christian history we
find God's revival fire being quenched by church leaders, many of
whom do it out of an ignorant zeal to 'protect' the gospel. More
often than not, they persecute that which they do not understand.
When things start happening that people have not experienced

before, it is easy to imagine danger. When miracles start to take place, it is easy to assume that they must be counterfeit. When God is using someone new, or in a more powerful way than he has used you, it is easy to jump to the conclusion that deception and bad motives are involved.

During the Welsh Revival of the early 1900s, God used a young man named Evan Roberts as the main instrument of blessing to a dry and thirsty nation. Most Welsh clergy of the day, however, strongly opposed Roberts's ministry, fearing the influence he would have on 'their' congregations. Several took out full-page advertisements in the newspapers denouncing him as a heretic and a swindler. Dozens of pastors put their signature to these slanderous attacks.

Today, Evan Roberts is fondly remembered around the world as the human vessel God used to bring revival to Wales one hundred years ago. Few can recall the name of even one of his detractors.

More recently, the Chinese house-church Christian Brother Yun, whose book *The Heavenly Man* has blessed hundreds of thousands of Christians and challenged them to a more committed walk with Christ, has also been the subject of severe criticism, slander and gossip. Many false accusations have been made against this humble servant of the Lord. Every one has proved to be nonsense, and yet the opposition from within some parts of the Body of Christ continues and many Christians are apt to believe the lie rather than discern the truth.

When fellow believers do what they can to stop the flow of God's blessing, they place themselves in a dangerous position. It would be far better if more Christians took the same patient attitude of the Pharisee Gamaliel, who wisely advised, 'Leave these men alone! Let them go! For if their purpose or activity is of human origin, it will fail. But if it is from God, you will not be able to stop these men; you will only find yourselves fighting against God' (Acts 5:38–39).

*   *   *   *   *   *

When the revival started in Nagaland, most Ao church leaders had not been expecting such a dramatic conviction of God to grip their communities. To their credit, many of them discerned that the revival was of God and not from the devil. They reasoned, with justification, that the devil never makes a person holy, never causes a believer to hunger and thirst for more of Jesus Christ and his word and never leads an individual to be born again. By examining the fruit of the revival, many Naga church leaders deduced that it was truly a visitation from God, and they were humble enough to accept it even though it had not originated in their own churches.

Others, however, mocked and feared the revival. Some Christians who had experienced the touch of the Holy Spirit were excommunicated. Others were beaten. A few were even killed.

When an evangelist named Chuba visited the village of Chiechama, dozens of Nagas were converted and baptized. Tragically, however, the local church rejected these new babes in Christ and refused to allow the revival preachers under their roof. On one occasion, the doors were locked to prevent the new believers from having a prayer meeting, but some young girls put their hands on the lock and prayed—and immediately the lock opened by itself![88]

In time, the new believers realized that the only option for them was to construct their own building and have separate services. One night, during a meeting, some Christians who opposed the revival came and set fire to it.

> All of the believers stood up and sang a song and came out of the church. Right after they came out, the roof of the church building burned and crashed down. In many places, church buildings were dismantled and burnt. Believers were severely persecuted. Even their properties were seized because of their faith.[89]

Hevukhu Achumi Sema recalled what happened when revival first broke out in the northern Sumi territory in 1960:

> A few members from my church attended prayer meetings in Changtongya and came back with their sins forgiven. When we saw these things we became suspicious and persecuted them by throwing stones at them, taking away their Bibles, beating them and many forms of torture.
>
> In spite of all these persecutions, the prayer group continued to pray for the people, loving them practically and helping the people in times of suffering and sickness. Despite their good deeds, persecution grew more intense against those who were filled with the Holy Spirit.
>
> One day our village joined together with three other surrounding villages. We took hold of 15 female revivalists, took off all their clothes and paraded them naked before all the people. We hoped to shame and humiliate them, but some of them said that even Jesus' clothes were removed when they crucified him, so they cheerfully received the humiliation and prayed for their persecutors.
>
> God started to use the revivalists through healings and within a few years the whole village was touched by the fire of revival. The people who were touched and filled with the Holy Spirit continually prayed for a great outpouring. God answered their prayers in 1976.[90]

In 1962, a revival meeting was conducted by a Rengma named Nethophumi at which seven members of the Ghokimi Baptist Church were present. All seven returned to their home village changed men. They started asking God to send revival, but their own congregation refused to let them pray inside the church. Undeterred, they continued to pray in their homes. More people joined them in calling out to heaven. There were about 60 families praying for revival, despite the stubborn resistance of the Baptist church. In August of that year, the leaders of the revival prayer meetings were fined 200 rupees each by the underground government, a huge amount of money in those days. Some of them were imprisoned and all kinds of underhand methods were used to try to stop the revival. In some cases, the persecution and torture were so severe that some revivalists even died.

In many places, Konyak believers were beaten and had their property confiscated and their crops stolen (though gradually the genuine love and goodness of these Christians broke down the resistance). Konyak villages were tightly controlled by the ahngs, who held all authority in social, political and religious matters. Whenever an ahng was convinced of the merits of Christianity, it was natural for the whole village to follow his lead, but in those places where the ahng opposed the gospel, darkness continued to rule. One such leader, a man named Mon, refused to allow his people to believe in Jesus. Many of his subjects wanted to become Christians,

> ... but he prevented them. How long could he oppose
> God? How long could he hinder people? Lightning struck
> his house twice in the year. Two main posts of his house,
> richly decorated with sacrificial offerings, were rent
> asunder. Sickness afflicted his family. The *ahng* began
> to feel shaky. He had a sense of fear and insecurity. He
> said, 'I cannot win by striving against God. Among my
> subjects, those who want to follow this new way of life are
> free to do so from now on.'[91]

Among the Angami, not all believers were willing to embrace the revival as a move of God. In 1962, Neihulie Angami was persecuted in the village of Mungchun, along with six other Christians he was travelling with. He recalls:

> We had a prayer meeting in a private house, as we were
> not welcome in the church. After the night service, as we

came out of the meeting, we were led away by a group of young men and were beaten and dragged out of the village. They left us in the jungle and went back to their village. We knelt down and prayed for them that God may forgive them and save them. As we prayed, the Holy Spirit of God moved our hearts in a wonderful way and we were all blessed. Peace and joy filled our hearts and we proceeded to another village.[92]

The split between the traditional Baptist churches and the revivalists had reached such proportions by the late 1950s that there seemed to be no hope of reconciliation. There were still some who preached that miracles had ended with the death of the last apostle in biblical days, despite the fact that the community right outside their church walls was witnessing many indisputable modern-day miracles and thousands of conversions.

Consequently, the Nagaland Christian Revival Church was formed in 1961. Large crowds of people flocked to the new churches. Often hundreds of people filled the pews and aisles of the church buildings and spilled out into the courtyard surrounding the church, as thousands of hungry and thirsty souls found their inner barrenness quenched by the living water of the Lord Jesus Christ.

Opposition to the awakening among the Nagas came in numerous ways and through countless people. A small revival had begun among the Zeliangrong in 1959 when local evangelistic teams set out to share Christ in animist villages. The Father of Lies saw the number of souls that were being lost to the Kingdom of God and made plans to disrupt God's work. A woman named Rani Gaidinliu started a movement that taught bizarre doctrines. Her teachings appealed to the nationalistic pride of the Zeliangrong and many were deceived.

This was a threat to the church. The followers of Gaidinliu worshipped her as a goddess for extraordinary and mysterious powers. Their programme was an attractive one, the very blueprint of a Naga heaven. They preached that the millennium was at hand. Her influence among the people was great.[93]

It was not until the late 1970s that her influence began to decline, but in the meantime Satan had succeeded in slowing down the growth of the Zeliangrong church. While revival burned brightly in most other Naga tribes, the Zeliangrong experienced only sporadic growth.

Despite the many years of persecution and resistance to the awakening in Nagaland, one church leader noted:

> Despite hindrances and severe opposition, the flame of revival continued to burn and floods of revival continued to flow like a big river ever increasing in depth and breadth. . . . By the grace and the wonderful work of God, the revival is still going strong and is now spreading into our neighbouring states and even beyond international boundaries.[94]

14

The 1960s & '70s: Amazing Grace

The first wave of revival swept through Nagaland in the 1950s. Hundreds of villages had been deeply affected by God's presence, but there still remained tens of thousands of unbelievers. At the start of the '60s, acceptance of the gospel across the territory was uneven. In some localities, entire villages had put their trust in the Son of God, but elsewhere many remained completely untouched. But the decade was to see further waves of mighty revival sweep across Nagaland. Many signs and wonders occurred and the church grew very strongly. A multitude of lives were changed by the blood of Jesus Christ as people repented and believed in God.

Neihulie Angami recalls that when he and his companions were at the village of Porambi in Phek District they saw a ball of fire fall from heaven into Lephuri on the India–Myanmar border. They rushed there and found that revival had broken out at this village even though no preacher had visited it. On another occasion, at the village of Phiro, the building where the believers were assembled was physically shaken by the power of God.[95]

The revival spread through all the Angami villages. This was accomplished not only by supernatural works of the Holy Spirit but also by the hard work of many Angami evangelists, who were spurred on over rugged mountain ranges and across dangerous rivers by the love of God in their hearts, seeking out those lost souls who had yet to hear that Jesus Christ died for their sins. One later reported:

The pain of the long journey on foot was unimaginable. There were no vehicular roads in existence to those villages. One had to walk across all the steep hills and deep gorges, the rugged and difficult terrains . . . with only long hanging cane-bridges swinging high over the deep blue rivers.[96]

By 1965, every Angami village in Nagaland had a church.

The revival also impacted the Ao with great power. During a convention at Keruma from January 5 to 8, 1961,

. . . the Spirit of God moved upon the people in a wonderful way. Many people . . . saw wonderful visions of angels coming down to the meeting place. Sunday morning Holy Communion was administered. The communion service began in the morning at about 8 o'clock and continued until 3:00 P.M. The presence of God was so real. . . . Everyone was so moved by the Spirit that people began to cry aloud in prayer. Even those who were serving the communion could not lift up their heads because of weeping. Prayer continued for hours.[97]

By the end of the '60s, the biggest problem facing many of the Naga churches was the lack of trained leadership. In 1965, only 25 of the 43 Yimchung churches had pastors. This lack of shepherds affected the flock.

Billy Graham's visit to Nagaland in November 1972 was a huge boost to the Naga church. More than 100,000 people came to Kohima to hear him. Some travelled for several days on foot through the jungle. With such a massive number of Christians from every tribe gathered in the city (whose population at the time was only about 30,000), the non-Christian Nagas were confronted with the reality of faith in Christ.

It was at this crusade that many Nagaland leaders and educated people dedicated their lives to Christ. The fire continued to burn till a dynamic movement of revival took place beginning from 1975 to this day.[98]

At the Gariphema New Village, prayer meetings were held between 1973 and 1977 that saw tremendous demonstrations of God's power. Many people were set free and born again into the Kingdom of God. But later on,

> . . . people began to murmur. . . . The Holy Spirit then spoke to the village again and said, 'If you don't believe my word, I am going to prove myself that you may know the truth. You shall not eat the fruit of your labour. There will be plagues upon your domestic animals also.' As the people were worried and pondered the warning, the judgement of God came upon the village. Paddy fields were destroyed by hailstorm. Those who had a very scanty harvest could not enjoy it because it turned very bitter and was unfit for human consumption. Even the animals refused to eat the paddy. This was soon followed by a plague which killed all the domestic animals. Ultimately the villagers realized their own shortcomings and the authenticity of the word of the Holy Spirit.[99]

In 1976, a second mighty wave of revival broke out in Nagaland and the whole state was taken captive by the power of the Holy Spirit. A 'spiritual awakening week' was organized from September 13 to 19 and five outstanding revival preachers were invited to speak at the Sumi Baptist Church. At 8 pm on the sixth day, a mighty visitation of the Holy Spirit took place. Hevukhu Achumi Sema recalls:

> Many people fell down to the floor in the Sumi Baptist Church and there were endless confessions of sin and ceaseless prayer and crying to the Lord. The prayer continued until 6 a.m. on Sunday 19th September 1976. . . . People started coming to the church every night for prayer and in the midst of these new and wonderful

experiences in the church, with new phenomena, a strong opposition arose from some of the church members. They said what was happening was contrary to Baptist doctrine. They took over the affairs of the church and locked out the born-again, Spirit-filled members from the church, including our pastor. I was one of the believers ostracized by the church. . . .

One night we were all praying and the Lord told us to go and pray inside the church. We went, but there was a large lock on the door of the church, so we stood outside and prayed to the Lord. While we were praying, one of the elders, Brother Mashito, came and said to me, 'Brother, the Lord told me to lay hands on the lock.' We prayed for him and when he laid his hands on the lock it fell down to the ground on its own accord. We entered the church and continued to pray. Nine young men who were half-drunk were sent by the opposition leaders to attack us. They waited outside the church with broken bottles in their hands. The Lord helped us by sending 24 police officers and we were not harmed.

After five months of prayer a new Sumi Baptist Church emerged which contained all the revived people. The new church building was completely finished within 40 days, which was a great miracle. God used the church to spread revival all over the region. Spreading the revival was the sole intense burden of our church.

In 1976, God's power also began to sweep through the dark Konyak villages and thousands of lives were transformed. At the start of this revival, the proportion of Christians among the Konyak was smaller than in other Naga tribes. There were 25,011 Christians (of whom 14,011 were baptized) in 1976 out of a total population of 69,790—just 36 per cent.[100] Such was the power of the revival in the late '70s that this percentage quickly grew as village after village was touched by God's presence and numerous miracles and signs and wonders took place.

A Naga publication outlined the state of the Konyak church before and after the impact of the awakening:

> Before the coming of these revivals, the church members were only nominal Christians. No one liked to volunteer for gospel work, as they did not have any missionary zeal. There was disunity among the people. Into this situation there broke a great revival in the whole of Nagaland in the early part of 1976, and its wave reached the Konyak churches too in the same year. . . . Many experienced a spiritual stir and started spreading the gospel from person to person, from family to family and from village to village.

> Remarkable changes have taken place among the Konyak because of this movement. According to the latest report [in 1981,] the Baptist church membership is 42,000 in the 103 organized churches. Of this a little over 25,000 were baptized during the last few years, which is something phenomenal in the history of the Konyak Baptist churches. The revival is still going on in all the places and many souls are being won to Christ. The great question is who will feed those thousands of new converts with the word of God. Many churches are in need of trained pastors to take up the responsibility.[101]

I will conclude this chapter with the words of Hopong, a Yimchung pastor in his seventies, recalling the visitation from the Lord that his tribe experienced:

> In the latter part of 1976, by the grace of God, revival broke out across many parts of Nagaland. Christians had been marginalized in our society until then, and those who tried to preach the gospel were strongly opposed and persecuted.

After God turned up in 1976, everything changed!

In the month of October 1976, there was a meeting in Muntum town. I went to the meeting and experienced the outpouring of the Holy Spirit. Before that day we didn't know anything about revival. Christianity to us was a set of rules and prohibitions. From that day on, Christianity became a living, powerful and intimate relationship with a wonderful Jesus.

When I arrived back home after the revival meeting I was filled with exceeding joy. My friends and family members came to see me, and all remarked that I seemed like a completely different person. That was true. Anyone who truly comes face to face with the Lord Jesus Christ will never be the same again.

When I preached in our church my message was altogether different than before. Now it came with great power and authority from the Holy Spirit. Many people were touched by the Lord and repented of their sins, but others were confused and opposed me. I found out then that during revival there is always great spiritual opposition. Those people who are willing to change their hearts and get off the roadway to death will be transformed, but those religious people who refuse to change and who strive to maintain the status quo soon become enemies of the revival—and the enemies of the people who advocate it.

I was threatened with excommunication from the church, and also told I would lose my job if I didn't stop preaching like I did. It was so strange to me because what had happened to me was not an act, or something I made up. Even my own brothers and sisters started hating me. When I visited their home they refused to offer me a cup of tea. On one occasion a man even came with a spear to kill me. I was beaten, but the Lord prevented him from ending my life.

I thank God that my wife and children continued to support me. Together we lifted up our hands and prayed for those who were opposing us.

I was banned from preaching, not only in our village church but also in surrounding villages that had previously welcomed me. Church leaders and village leaders slandered me and did all they could to drive me away. But we stayed and continued to trust in the Lord. When they locked the door of the church so I couldn't get inside, I just stood outside the door and prayed and worshipped the Lord with tears in my eyes.

Then the Lord started to work in wonderful ways. In a nearby village lived a seven-year-old boy with a terminal illness. When I prayed for him the Lord instantly healed him. Other miracles started taking place and many of the people who had opposed me now came and asked forgiveness.

I started holding evening Bible studies and many people came, believed in the Lord and were baptized. Suddenly the name of the Lord was prospering and the revival fire spread rapidly. By 1979 God had done such a great work that more than one thousand Yimchung people were baptized in a single day.

During the most intense times of the revival people would cry out and confess their sins in great anguish. They just had to get right with God as their pain and burden of sin was so great that another minute away from the embrace of Jesus Christ was too much for them to bear. Many times people fell to the ground under the power of the Holy Spirit. Others were prostrated and could not move. In each meeting people were shouting their sins to the Lord, all at the same time. They didn't care what the person next to them was doing—all that mattered was that people's hearts were surrendered to God.

15

A Change of Heart

The temptation seemed to be always, as today, toward
empty manifestation. This does not require any particular
cross, or death to the self-life. Hence it is always popular.
But there is only one safe, honest course to pursue with
the 'old man.' Bury him under six feet of earth, with his
face downward. The harder he scratches the deeper he
will go.

Frank Bartleman

The man whose little sermon is 'Repent' sets himself
against his age, and will for the time being be battered
mercilessly by the age whose moral tone he challenges.
There is but one end for such a man—'off with his head!'
You had better not try to preach repentance until you
have pledged your head to heaven.

Joseph Parker

It has been said that the depth of any revival will be determined
by the spirit of repentance that it generates. Indeed, it could be
said that by definition a revival has to contain repentance, as the
meaning of the word implies change: changed hearts, changed
lives, changed churches and even changed nations. A believer or
church that cannot see the need to alter the status quo is either
already living in revival or unaware of the need for repentance.

All the old revival preachers, be they Graham, Sunday, Moody,
Finney, Whitfield, Wesley, Peter, Paul or John the Baptist, had a
strong message of repentance. The great theologian A W Tozer
has said,

The old cross slew men; the new cross entertains them. The old cross condemned; the new cross amuses. The old cross destroyed confidence in the flesh; the new cross encourages it. . . . The flesh, smiling and confident, preaches and sings about the cross; before the cross it bows and toward that cross it points with carefully staged histrionics—but upon that cross it will not die, and the reproach of the cross it stubbornly refuses to bear.

It could be pointed out that there have been some 'revivals' in Western countries in recent years where there was little evidence of repentance. Instead of people feeling ill about their sin and selves, they have been encouraged to feel good about themselves. Instead of being instructed to believe in God, they are told that God believes in them! However, deep repentance of sin has certainly been one of the dominant features of the Naga revivals of the past 50 years.

During the 1940s, revival had been more necessary than ever as the social and moral climate of Nagaland changed for the worse. During the Second World War, the Nagas were

> . . . exposed to the outside world [and] in many ways this had affected their spiritual and moral life. . . . Robbery, adultery, drunkenness, dishonesty, etc. became common in Nagaland. . . . After the war, Christians became worldly, lukewarm and indifferent to God. The spiritual life had touched the lowest ebb. Revival was, therefore, the need of the Church.[102]

The conditions for that revival were created by the impact of war and extreme hardship during the 1950s. Edward Singa recalls:

> Human misery led people to seek God. Many villages were burned and reburned; people were left homeless. They had to rush to the jungle for security. . . . The people were the grain between two grind-stones—the Indian army and the Naga independence force. The only

solution, people thought, was to seek for spiritual peace and security.[103]

Neihulie Angami recalled how the 1950s revival among the Nagas began:

> The real breakthrough . . . came when the people turned from their wicked ways and sought the face of God in fervent prayers. And when the Spirit of God moved upon the people they began to see their sinful condition and their unworthiness before the Lord. The conviction of sin was so heavy upon the people that weeping and loud confessions of sin and prayers were heard on every side. Drunkards, gamblers and the worst of sinners were wonderfully transformed. Everywhere people began to repent and make restitutions. Long-time enemies were reconciled and they began to love one another in the Lord. Divorced couples were reunited and broken hearts were healed.[104]

In the 1950s, the Christian population increased significantly in every Naga tribe. How did this spectacular growth take place among people who many considered hostile to the gospel just a few years earlier? It was, quite simply, a move of God: the Holy Spirit turned up in their midst in great power and love, convicting people of sin, righteousness and judgement. The Naga church historian Phuveyi Dozo remembers what happened when a revival preacher named Solomon visited the village of Runguze in 1958:

> Revival began, and every night a tarry-meeting was conducted. People were convicted of their sins, crying, weeping and confessing. . . . The village was filled with revival songs and prayers. People rushed to church daily. They forgot about their crops for months, but lost nothing. Many non-Christians rushed to church to see what was going on—village leaders, fathers, mothers,

young people and children were coming more and more. They used to surround the church walls and looked over to see what was happening. To their surprise, they saw their children and relatives there praying for them. Every night many non-Christians used to slip into the church to join the Christians. . . . Family by family moved into the church. They persuaded their non-Christian neighbours to come and join them. . . . Today this entire village has become a Christian village.[105]

Zhowhuyi is one Chakhesang Christian leader who has lived through the revival years. Looking back, he reminisces about the effects God's Spirit had on his tribe's church and society:

In the beginning some Christian leaders were uncertain about the whole thing and wondered if the revival originated from God or the devil. We watched closely to see what would happen.

One of the first things that happened was that the Lord started revealing the sins of each person, specifically and powerfully. Grown men and women and young boys and girls together were convicted of their sins in extraordinary ways that only God could orchestrate. Many anguished cries and tears of repentance and confession were shed as people longed to be in right standing with God. Many sins of stealing, adultery, murder, and encroaching on neighbours' boundaries were confessed publicly and restitution was made wherever possible. This characteristic of deep repentance of sin convinced many leaders that this move truly was from God. The devil never causes any person to repent of his or her sins and seek after Jesus Christ!

After confession and prayer, many people would rise from their knees completely free from their past and with new, shiny hearts fully devoted to God. Great joy and peace washed over our souls. Suddenly the boring endurance tests that used to be our prayer meetings became times of great enthusiasm to be eagerly looked forward to.

Many prayer meetings continued for five hours, and nobody was tired. People were completely overwhelmed with deep joy and awe of God. Even people who had been greedy and selfish a short time before were now willing to give their homes and properties to someone else who may need it more than they did.

The devil tried to interfere and stop this work of God but the Holy Spirit himself warned us of the devil's plans in advance and even showed us through visions what the enemy was trying to do. The church would come together in united prayer and each obstacle was overcome.

Over the years there have been many attacks, but we have found if our focus is on the Lord then we shall walk in victory as the Lord determines. One day I went to a village and two men came out and attempted to kill me by slashing me with their *daos* [Naga machetes formerly used for head-hunting]. The men surrounded me on each side, but the moment they raised their *daos* in the air to kill me the Spirit of the Lord caused their weapons to fly out of their hands and I was safe.

The Church continued to grow among our people, as the power and light of the gospel penetrated to every village and community.[106]

16

Binding the Strongman

*'When a strong man, fully armed, guards his own
house, his possessions are safe. But when someone
stronger attacks and overpowers him, he takes
away the armour in which the man trusted and
divides up the spoils.'*

Luke 11:21–22

There is a war between the saint and Satan, and that so
bloody a one that the cruellest which ever was fought by
men will be found but sport and child's play to this. . . .
The stage whereon this war is fought is every man's soul.

William Gurnell (1616–1679)

The light of the gospel was burning so brightly across Nagaland
during the revival years that the darkness residing in men's hearts
and the demonic forces that bound their communities were
banished.

For centuries, the Naga tribes had been enslaved to demonic
powers. Head-hunting was one way this influence was manifested,
as plainly described in the following account by the Ao evangelist
Kijunglaba, who visited the large village of Tuensang in December
1936:

We found almost all the men were heavy drinkers
and most of the women were unhealthy [ie had sexual
diseases], especially the young girls. A boy about seven
years of age was holding a snake about three feet long.
. . . Some elders said that Christianity was good for
women and slaves, but not for men. They said that

their social customs and culture could not go well with
Christianity. . . .

Suddenly my attention was diverted to some men running
to and fro and in no time they started beating the war
log-drum. To me it was only a sound but to the people at
Tuensang and for the surrounding villages it was of great
significance. . . . The men were returning with enemies'
heads. . . . Excitement ran high among the people and
the very moment indicated that their hearts were full of
joy beyond unspeakable. Dancing, singing and drinking
started, men in full warrior-dress could be seen moving
in a very excited mood, challenging the enemies. Even
the children were very much alerted for the occasion
and no feeling of sympathy was expressed for the people
and the relatives of those who had lost their lives. I
never witnessed such a glorious occasion in my life. I
felt as if the whole village and the earth on which I was
standing were shaking out of joy. The head-hunters with
two heads—one [of] a man and the other of a woman—
arrived at the village. . . .

The procession was magnificent and the men who
participated in the head-hunting were half drunk but still
they had the sense to realize that they were receiving the
highest honour. They could utter only a few words: 'Yes,
we are the tigers; we have the power to get up through
the enemies' defence and fetch our trophies! Yes, we are
the hawks; we can swoop down like lightning from the
sky and can snatch our enemies before they notice!' . . .
People would come in front of the heads and say mocking
words. 'What was your dream last night? Tell us, have you
come to visit our village?'

Darkness was approaching but to them there was no
darkness. Men and women went mad with joy, forgetting
their homes. Young girls moved here and there,
challenging their lovers to become real men by bringing

home enemies' heads. To them it was a most glorious night but . . . we had experienced the saddest night. . . . The longest night was over and the day was at hand when these head-hunters would see a new day in Christ.[107]

For many head-hunters, that new day came in dramatic circumstances. In 1971, the field director of the Yimchung Baptist Association noted:

Last year, 1970, was a special year for the famous head-hunters in the Yimchung area. Now they surrendered before our Lord Jesus Christ, becoming his servants, abandoning all old tasks. Once they were the instruments of Satan; now they are instruments of Christ Jesus.[108]

Before the 1970s, the Yimchung area was described as a 'paradise' for head-hunters. A gruesome harvest of human life was reaped. One Yimchung warrior had 42 heads in his collection, another 50, a third 60 and another 62. Thongpong was the warrior who had taken 50 human heads and he had decorated his house with them. He came to Christ after narrowly escaping death in a fight, and all things became new in his life. Wongto and Chanchi, from the villages of Wongpong and Aiponger respectively, were other head-hunters who found Christ.

As Christianity took hold among people whose minds had been so darkened by demonic powers, confrontation between the light of the gospel and the prevailing darkness was inevitable. On many occasions, demon-possessed people tried to stop the revival. The Christians, almost all of whom had been conservative Baptists with no experience of how to deal with such things, had to learn quickly. On one occasion, when believers came together to fast and pray for the whole of Nagaland,

Many great deliverances took place. Once a demon-possessed man was brought to the prayer centre. The man was so possessed and tormented by demons that he was uncontrollable and had to be bound with chains.

One day he broke the chains and ran away. It took several strong men to control him and bring him back to the prayer centre. He remained there for many days. Those who had dedicated themselves to the ministry of prayer spent many days in fasting and prayer for him, and God gloriously delivered him. Now he is of sound mind and goes from church to church giving his testimony of what God has done for him.[109]

At the start of the 1950s revival, many Nagas were still animists, worshipping the spirits and demons their ancestors had worshipped for countless centuries. The Naga Christians banded together and determined to fast and pray until the Holy Spirit removed all the demonic strongholds that were keeping people from acknowledging the truth of Jesus Christ.

In Sendenyu, the Christians prayed and fasted for 15 days, crying out to God and binding the works of the devil. On the 15th day, three strange and dramatic events took place, witnessed by many people. First, outside the village, on a hill the Rengma called Temi Thyükenko Thun ('Mount for Drying Human Flesh'), there was a large cave known as Demon's Cave, where the villagers believed Satan roasted human flesh. On this day, the cave simply collapsed, so that no one could ever enter it again.

They found the stone rolled away.

Luke 24:2

On the plain between the two rivers the Nyeshweru and the Temejochon, there stood a huge rock that locals believed was a sacred spiritual stronghold. People were afraid to go near it—no one dared even to cultivate the land around it, for fear of evil consequences. Local legend taught (and experience confirmed) that anyone who went near the rock would return home gravely ill, and some people had died. The rock was so large and heavy that any number of people could not possibly have budged it from its location if they had tried. It weighed many tons.

On the same day the Demon's Cave collapsed, the local people were astonished to find that the huge rock on the plain had simply disappeared. They searched high and low for it, but no trace of it could be found. Today, the Nagas grow crops on the land they were previously too afraid to go near.

He removed the foreign altars and the high places, smashed the sacred stones and cut down the Asherah poles.

2 Chronicles 14:3

During head-hunting days, when few Nagas knew the Lord, the village elders of Sendenyu planted three wild rubber trees, known as Chin Bin, at the entrance to the village. Over the decades, these grew to an enormous height and their tops joined together so that the three looked like one gigantic tree. The villagers ascribed spiritual power to them and so ancestor worship and other rituals were conducted there. Whenever their warriors went on head-hunting expeditions, they hung the severed heads of their victims from the branches of these trees. In their language, the villagers called this triple tree Rüpe Bin, which means 'Tree for Hanging Human Heads'.

On the same day the Lord destroyed the Demon Cave and the large rock disappeared, Rüpe Bin fell to the ground with a great crash.

All over Nagaland, in a myriad different ways, the spiritual opposition to Christ's rule was being eroded. Satan had been defeated by Christ on the Cross and now he was being defeated throughout Nagaland. As the strongman was bound and his influence diminished, the way was prepared for the Naga church to 'take away the armour in which he trusted and divide up the spoils'.

17

Touched, Purified, Established: the Last 25 Years

By the dawn of the 1980s, the Naga church was spiritually strong and zealous to reach the lost. The revivals of the 1970s had deeply affected every aspect of Naga society. Probably every village in Nagaland contained a church. The '80s and the years that followed could be characterized as a time when God purified and established the church in Nagaland, grounding the believers in his word and forming them into mature Christians.

Although it is generally recognized that there has been no widespread revival in Nagaland since the 1970s, there have been regular reminders of God's love and grace, manifested in diverse ways. Pastor Liegise remembers when six Naga preachers walked to Hafflong, in Assam, in 1982:

> They walked along mountain trails to get there, but on the way back from preaching they got lost. The night fell and they were now stumbling around in the darkness. One of the men was sick and dehydrated. He said if he didn't get water to drink soon he would die of thirst. The others searched around as well as they could but because it was in the mountains they could find no water to quench his thirst.
>
> In their desperate situation they all knelt down in the jungle and prayed to God, asking for his help. Suddenly a fountain appeared near them, springing up from the ground! All of them drank until they were full and lay down on the ground in the mountains and slept. The next

morning they awoke and searched for the fountain, but it had disappeared.

They prayed and the Lord showed them the correct path to take out of the mountains and they continued on their way full of joy.[110]

To the present day the fires of revival among the Sumi Nagas continue to be fanned. The young people are taught the word of God and encouraged to seek after the Lord Jesus with all their heart. As Hevukhu Achumi Sema says,

> Thanks to the mercy of God, thousands of Sumi people have been touched, purified, established and trained over the decades since God sovereignly decided to pour out his Spirit on our area.[111]

The Konyak church continued to grow throughout the 1980s and '90s, and the spiritual life of Konyak Christians generally remained strong compared with some of the other tribes, where the fire of the Holy Spirit may have burned less brightly than they did in the late 1970s. The Bangkok-based Christian organization Ethnos Asia has published an account by a Naga evangelist named Ahao, who walked from Myanmar to eastern Nagaland in order to reach out to the Konyak. His testimony displays the zeal and commitment typical of many Naga evangelists.

> A few years ago we went to visit our brothers in eastern Nagaland. Because they were head-hunters, we couldn't take the main roads and instead we walked two months through the jungle to reach them. When we arrived, they came out to meet us and laughed at us because we were fully dressed and they were naked.

> We followed them into the village and were shocked to see their living conditions. They lived in long houses with no walls or windows, only a roof reaching down to the ground. The dead were left outside to rot in the

air. The people had no doctors or medicine and were
suffering from many diseases. They were living in
complete darkness; the message of salvation had not been
heard and Christ was not preached. When we saw these
conditions, we began to cry. God had given us a difficult
task, but we began to pray and fast for wisdom and
strength.

God answered our prayers and helped us to reach the
people. . . . After three years of prayer and fasting and
tears, we have planted many churches and have built
many schools. There has been a revival and many have
been filled with the Holy Spirit.

When they received Christ, the people said to us: 'You are
a very different tribe, but now you are our brothers and
sisters. Naga people, why did you come here so late? Now
that you have opened our eyes we can see what is good
and what is bad, so please don't leave us. Stay with us!'[112]

The Konyak in Nagaland today have the distinction of having
the highest percentage of Christians of any Naga tribe. In 1997,
114,185 out of 115,039 Konyak in Nagaland were Christians—99.3
per cent of the population.[113] This tribe, once feared as vicious
head-hunters, have been the grateful recipients of a spiritual
blessing instigated by Jesus Christ, the Lover of their souls. They
have responded in large numbers to the love and grace of God,
and entire communities have been transformed from the inside
out.

Among some tribes, such as the Yimchung, the gospel had
arrived only in the 1950s and so was still relatively new even in the
early '80s. Pastor Hopong testifies to its recent advance among his
tribe:

During one worship meeting in Kiussor village in 1983,
suddenly everyone saw—with their eyes wide open—a
vision of a ladder coming down from heaven with angels

ascending and descending on it. It was as if the roof of our church building was lifted off and we all saw this remarkable and humbling sight.

We know that the revival was a work of God because people's lives were being drastically transformed from darkness to light—from bondage to liberty. Broken marriages were put back together, drug addicts and alcoholics were completely set free, and people who had stolen from their neighbours—sometimes years beforehand—went back and asked forgiveness and made restitution. Only a genuine work of the Lord can bring such results!

Not all the leaders who had originally opposed the revival changed their positions however. Some of them suddenly died and others became paralyzed or were struck down with incurable sicknesses. God was gracious to these leaders, and by bringing them to a place of utter weakness, some of them humbled themselves, confessed their sins, and repented.

So many people wanted to find the Lord that it was pointless trying to conduct meetings in the church buildings, so we started holding open-air evangelistic meetings where hundreds, and occasionally thousands, of people gathered together.

Our meetings continued for many hours at a time and countless people met the Living Christ. Straight away almost all of these new believers wanted to go and preach the word of God to the lost. It wasn't something we had to teach, it was automatic. When God took possession of a person it was natural for that person to have the same desires and vision that God has—and his vision is to reach the lost and display his love for all mankind.

Often we entered villages where warriors came out and confessed how many people they had killed during head-hunting raids. The human skulls were still hanging from trees. In each village there was one special tree set aside for heads to be hung, like macabre trophies. These men came with tears in their eyes and asked forgiveness from the Lord Jesus for their sins.

One of the main characteristics of our meetings during this time was when God would speak through a prophecy, exposing the secret sin of a person and warning them of dire consequences if they would not confess that specific sin and repent. Most people would be melted in their heart and would hand their sin to the Lord, but on a number of occasions people who continued to plead innocence were immediately struck down and died, according to the prophecy that had been given to them.

As the years passed in the 1980s the fires of revival gradually died down among the Yimchung, until the embers that once burned white-hot contained just a little warmth. Our churches were still full, but we had walked away from the Lord and had started doing things in our own strength. The memory of the revival in the late 1970s had changed our lives so drastically that we could never turn our backs on the Lord, but we lost our first love.

I believe the main reasons why we lost the revival fires were firstly because people went back to their sin, and [secondly] because of a lack of good, systematic biblical teaching in our churches. We did our best to teach and train new Bible teachers, but sheep need constant feeding, not just from time to time.

Although the spiritual fervour was waning in some places, throughout the 1990s and up to the present time churches the length and breadth of Nagaland have been packed with worshippers. In 1997, the India Mission Association conducted the first thorough survey of Nagaland for many years,[114] and found that out of a total population of 887,736 Nagas, 767,804 were Christians—an astonishing 86.5 per cent. The lowest concentration of believers was among the Kuki, but even of them 70.8 per cent were Christians.

The name of Jesus Christ has certainly been glorified throughout Nagaland!

18

What Now?

A revival will cease whenever Christians become
mechanical in their attempts to promote it. When their
faith is strong, and their hearts are warm and mellow, and
their prayers full of holy emotion, and their words with
power, then the work goes on. But when their prayers
begin to be cold and without emotion, and they begin
to labor mechanically, and to use words without feeling,
then the revival will cease.

Charles Finney, 1837

During a ministry trip to Britain in the autumn of 1998, I found
myself with a spare day before my evening flight back to Asia
departed from Heathrow Airport. I decided to drive to Wales
and visit the site of the great Welsh Revival of 1903–05. Since the
time I was a young Christian I had been fascinated by accounts
of this revival, which swept around the world bringing salvation
to millions. I marvelled at how God had chosen a young, single
man, Evan Roberts, as his instrument to shake a whole nation.
The power of God had so stirred communities in Wales that
people walking to meetings sometimes had to stop a few blocks
away from the church, take hold of a post and pray for strength to
continue because the conviction of God was so strong.

Thousands of rough coal-miners were so transformed in
their habits that the pit ponies were unable to understand their
commands any more—they had become used to harsh swear
words and curses and could not recognize the gentle new words
coming from the miners' mouths. Multitudes of people in Wales
were being truly born again and experiencing a new heart in Jesus

Christ. The Welsh police force had nothing to do except form themselves into worship groups and travel around the country singing praises to God!

I drove to Loughour in southern Wales. This was Evan Roberts's home town, from which the revival had radiated out all across the country. I managed to locate Moriah Chapel, where the Holy Spirit fell in great power during the revival. The gates and doors of this historic building were padlocked, but I was able to telephone an elderly caretaker, who kindly came and opened it up for me. It was a wonderful experience to hear some of her stories as we toured the 800-seat chapel, which a century earlier had nightly overflowed with eager crowds of people.

I asked her how many people attended the services there now. 'Oh, you would be disappointed,' she replied, and changed the subject. When another opportunity arose in our conversation, I asked again. This time I received a reluctant answer. 'Between 10 and 12 people come on most Sunday mornings. We haven't had enough members to have our own pastor for the past 30 years,' she lamented.

I came to realize that it is not enough for us to experience God only in the past. As someone has said, 'God has no grandchildren.' He must become a daily reality in our lives and communities. When he fed the Children of Israel in the wilderness, they were unable to store the manna overnight. Those who tried to eat it the next day found it had turned rotten. In the same way, our spiritual lives must be renewed every single day. This principle applies to individuals, families, churches and even whole nations. We cannot live off yesterday's blessings. God's mercies are 'new every morning' (Lamentations 3:23).

Today, the young people of Loughour have no knowledge of the gospel. Most of them don't even know who Evan Roberts was or what happened in the very chapel they walk past every day on their way to school.

How about the Naga church? Is it still growing in grace, trusting God for its daily sustenance? Or are the blessings of the revival years merely becoming distant memories in the annals of its history?

*   *   *   *   *   *

In the 1970s, the Naga church made a commitment to send 10,000 cross-cultural missionaries to unreached tribes and ethnic groups throughout Asia. Many have gone to places as far-flung as Indonesia, the Philippines, China and Japan. Hundreds have crossed Nagaland's borders into Myanmar and into many Indian states such as Assam and Arunachal Pradesh, which are home to dozens of unevangelized tribes.

In most places, these missionaries have proved to be highly effective. They are tough people who can walk over high mountains and through deep valleys in search of lost souls and can live frugally on much less than the average Western missionary. Still, at the present time, the original objective of sending 10,000 missionaries is not close to being reached.[115]

If the Naga church is ever able to train and send that many missionaries out into the dark regions surrounding them, the impact would be immense. More than one thousand unreached people-groups live in the stretch of land from Pakistan through northern India, Nepal, Bhutan, Myanmar, Thailand, Vietnam and Laos. Hundreds of these groups are similar to the Nagas in appearance, culture and language. Satan knows this, and is working to ensure that it doesn't happen.

In many areas of Nagaland, it has now been almost 25 years since the last sustained revival of God. How has the Naga church fared? Is its spiritual life still strong and vibrant or has time gradually made Jesus less real in the midst of the Nagas, as seems to have happened in so many parts of the world that revival has visited?

The modernization of Naga society has introduced new challenges for the Naga church. Hevukhu Achumi Sema, the director of the Nagaland Missionary Movement, has written:

> The growth of urban areas marked the beginning of migration from the rural areas to towns. Village unity began to disintegrate and with it church discipline became more complicated.
>
> The new Nagaland Government started issuing liquor licences all over the state. Things like radio, television and movies had bad effects, especially on the young people in urban areas. Many people started drinking alcohol heavily, and many homes were broken because of alcoholism. Many young people started using drugs which came from Myanmar via Manipur State and some of the young people became drug addicts when they went out of Nagaland for study.
>
> Before the modernization came into the land, people were honest and robbery was unknown except for a few cases. The house doors in the villages were not locked when the people went to work in the fields. Adultery was rare and the people were very simple in their faith. The spiritual and moral lives of the people were equally good and the community life of the village was strong. Many Christians lost their interest in church attendance, prayer and Bible study. With the influx of money, alcohol, drugs, movies and Western fashions etc, many people became backslidden and the moral and spiritual life of the church declined.[116]

In recent years, I have been both greatly blessed and deeply concerned during my travels in Nagaland. On the one hand, the deep love and appreciation I feel for Naga Christians is sincere. They are among the most Bible-literate, pure and honest I have had the privilege to meet. Perhaps only among China's house-church congregations have I met believers with the same fervency and hunger for God's word I have encountered in Nagaland.

But on the other hand I have also seen how the Naga church is struggling in many areas, and signs of spiritual decay have set in. This sad cycle of repentance, revival and backsliding seems to have occurred to the Israelites throughout the Scriptures, and throughout history to peoples and nations that have experienced revival.

Naga pastors have expressed their deep concern to me about the present state of the church in Nagaland, but few seem to know where the cause of the problem lies, or what to do about it. When a doctor is unable accurately to diagnose an ailment in one of his regular patients, he often asks for a second opinion. From a vantage point a little further removed, another doctor is often able to see the problem much more clearly. In the same way, it is possible that outsiders may be able to help the Naga church to see where it is heading better than the Nagas can themselves. In my opinion, the main factor that has contributed to the demise of spiritual life among the Nagas is one that many Christians may not understand: I mean the institutionalization of the Naga church.

Revival first broke out in Nagaland after all the foreign missionaries were expelled. Afraid that the large harvest could be lost unless more pastors and teachers were raised up, the Naga church sent dozens of young men away to attend Bible colleges and seminaries in central and southern India, Singapore and Hong Kong, and even as far away as America and Britain. Everywhere I have travelled in Nagaland I have met church leaders who are 'Reverend Doctors'. It may seem strange to find someone with a doctorate of theology ministering in a church on the edge of a remote jungle, but these young men, out of their love for God, spent six or seven years of their lives in seminary acquiring knowledge so that they could be the leaders of the Naga church in this generation.

Yet the revival fire of God is missing from most Naga churches today. The perception has been lost that the way to spread the gospel is for villagers to open their mouths and tell their neighbours what Jesus has done in their hearts. Christianity has become a religious duty for many in Nagaland rather than a passion. Many look to their pastors and not to the Holy Spirit for direction and comfort.

Religiosity is closely related to control. As the Naga church evolved along strict denominational lines, every initiative by believers that did not come directly under the control of 'the church' was shunned and often was regarded as worthless and rebellious. I know of one small mission that has dozens of young Christians lining up to join with hearts ablaze for Jesus and a passion to go anywhere to take the gospel to the unreached. Does the institutional Naga church as a whole support and encourage this mission? Certainly not! The Baptist hierarchy could never help to build up a work that is not under its control. While huge sums of money in Nagaland are spent on church buildings and pastors' salaries, these young men and women who desire to give themselves to frontline missionary service cannot even raise 500 rupees—about US$10—a month in support from their home churches and communities.

When God's people become so blind that they fail to see any worth in activities that thrill the heart of God but spend their time, energies and resources on things of little eternal consequence, a spiritual rot has already set in. Those churches are on a dangerous slope of decline. D M Panton, a British pastor, once defined revival as 'the inrush of the Spirit into the body that threatens to become a corpse'. While it is certainly too soon to suggest that the Naga church is threatening to become a corpse, it is not as warm-blooded as it once was.

May Nagaland not find itself 100 years from now as spiritually barren and devoid of life as once-blessed Wales is today! In this crucial stage in its history, as exposure to the outside world increases all the time, the Naga church is stagnating, in danger of becoming a mire of dead religiosity. May the Nagas reflect on their history and realize that it is only through the power of the Lord Jesus Christ—he who rules the world with truth and grace and holds all authority in heaven and on earth—that they even exist as a people today!

And so we come to the end of our look at Christianity among the Nagas. Their journey has been a remarkable one. They have walked through the valley of the shadow of death and have been the victims of unspeakable cruelty, yet they have also experienced the heights of God's greatness and power like few peoples in history. In their darkest hour, God himself came down from heaven and walked with the Nagas hand in hand, helping them through the valley to a place of honour, humility and deep dignity.

I close with this poignant quote from Kaka Iralu:

> It is an obvious fact that we have been able to survive these fifty years of oppression and persecution only because of the sustaining grace of Jesus Christ whom we have accepted as our Lord and Saviour—that is, in spite of all our hypocrisy and our failures. The Naga story would have perished long ago without Christ; neither would there be any future Naga story without him.[117]

The Nagas did not find their true dignity in themselves, their ethnic roots, their head-hunting or the defence of their homeland. They discovered it in the person and life of Jesus Christ, the Living and One True God.

Notes

1. See Joseph S Thong, *Head-Hunters Culture (Historic Culture of Nagas)* (Tseminyu, Nagaland: Joseph S Thong, 1997), pp2–3.

2. John Henry Hutton, *The Angami Nagas: with Some Notes on Neighbouring Tribes* (London: Macmillan, 1921)

3. Thong, *Head-Hunters Culture*, pii

4. Ibid, p11

5. Ibid, p10

6. Ibid, pii

7. Puthuvail Thomas Philip, *The Growth of Baptist Churches in Nagaland* (Gauhati: Christian Literature Centre, 1976), p12

8. Ibid, pp11–12

9. Thong, *Head-Hunters Culture*, pp17–18

10. Kaka D Iralu, *Nagaland and India, the Blood and the Tears: A Historical Account of the 52 Years Indo–Naga War and the Story of Those Who Were Never Allowed to Tell It*, a book published privately in Nagaland, September 2000, p239

11. Philip, *The Growth of Baptist Churches*, pp47–48

12. V H Sword, *Baptists in Assam* (Chicago: Conference Press, 1935), p63

13. John Butler, 'A Sketch of Assam', 1847, pp149–52; cited in Verrier Elwin (ed), *The Nagas in the Nineteenth Century* (London: Oxford University Press, 1969), pp515–16

14. Philip, *The Growth of Baptist Churches*, p50. Because this man did not belong to a village inside Naga territory proper, many Naga Christians today do not regard Hube's conversion as the first fruit of Christianity among the Nagas. The conversion of the Ao Nagas in 1872 is generally viewed as the birth of the Naga church.

15. Ibid, p51

16. Ibid, p51

17. Ibid, pp51–52

18. Ibid, p52

19. Ibid, pp52–53

20. Ibid, p53

21. Bendangyabang A Ao, *History of Christianity in Nagaland: A Source Material* (Mokokchung: Shalom Ministry, 1998), p151

22. Philip, *The Growth of Baptist Churches*, p55

23. M M Clark, *A Corner in India* (Philadelphia: American Baptist Publication Society, 1907), p14

24. Philip, *The Growth of Baptist Churches*, p57

25. Letter from S W Rivenburg, July 2, 1891, cited in Ao, *History of Christianity in Nagaland*, p128

26. There are many other Naga tribes living in other states of India such as Arunachal Pradesh, Assam and Manipur, as well as in the neighbouring country of Myanmar (Burma). However, the accounts and statistics in this chapter are restricted to the 13 Naga tribes that live in the state of Nagaland.

27. *The Missionary Magazine* LXIII (1887), p346

28. *The Assam Baptist Conference* (Session VII, 1904–05), p57

29. Philip, *The Growth of Baptist Churches*, p98

30. Ibid, pp80–81

31. Ibid, p84

32. Ibid, p90

33. See Narola Rivenburg (ed), *The Star of the Naga Hills: Letters from Rev. Sidney and Hattie Rivenburg, Pioneer Missionaries in Assam 1883–1923* (Philadelphia: Judson Press, 1941).

34. Phuveyi Dozo, *The Growth of the Baptist Church in Chakhesang Naga Tribe (India)* (Pasadena: Fuller Theological Seminary, thesis, 1978), pp30–31

35. Ibid, p40

36. Philip, *The Growth of Baptist Churches*, p117
37. Ibid, p124
38. Ibid, p104
39. Sword, *Baptists in Assam*, p115
40. Ibid, p115
41. Philip, *The Growth of Baptist Churches*, p105
42. Ibid, p109
43. Ibid, p50
44. Dr O M Rao, *Longri Ao: A Biography* (Nagaland, nd), p32
45. Ibid, pp30–31
46. Ibid, p33
47. Philip, *The Growth of Baptist Churches*, pp155–56
48. Dozo, *The Growth of the Baptist Church*, p103
49. Philip, *The Growth of Baptist Churches*, pp161–62
50. Interview with Hopong, Kohima, 2002
51. Philip, *The Growth of Baptist Churches*, pp158–59
52. See Tajen Ao, *British Occupation of Naga Country* (Kohima: Naga Literature Society, 1993), and Piketo Sema, *British Policy and Administration in Nagaland 1881–1947* (New Delhi: Scholar Publishing House, 1991).
53. Philip, *The Growth of Baptist Churches*, pp18–19
54. For more information, see Arthur Swinson, *The Battle of Kohima* (New York: Stein & Day, 1967), and John Colvin, *Not Ordinary Men: The Story of the Battle of Kohima* (Barnsley, UK: Pen & Sword, 2004).
55. Field Marshal Sir William Slim, *Defeat into Victory* (London: Four Square Books, 1958), pp336–37
56. Letter to Sir Winston Churchill, dated March 28, 1947
57. Iralu, *Nagaland and India*, p69–70
58. Ibid, p80
59. Ibid, pp82–83

60. Ibid, p85

61. Ibid, p90

62. Ibid, pp98–99

63. Ibid, pp229–31

64. Ibid, pp231–32

65. Ibid, pp7–8

66. Philip, *The Growth of Baptist Churches*, p183

67. From an unpublished report by Hevukhu Achumi Sema, director of the Nagaland Missionary Movement

68. Iralu, *Nagaland and India*, p444

69. Most of the testimonies in this chapter come from the booklet by Joseph S Thong, *Miracles of the Holy Spirit* (Kohima: Sendenyu Baptist Church, 1995) and from an earlier report, *Sendenyu Revival Silver Jubilee: February 1959–February 1984*. This citation is from Thong, pp75–81.

70. Personal communication with a Naga Christian leader, September 2003

71. 'The Revivals and the Response', unpublished report, pp31–32

72. Neihulie Angami, *A Brief Account of Nagaland Revivals and the Formation of Nagaland Christian Revival Church* (NCRC, 1987), pp7–8

73. Nagaland Christian Revival Church, 'Go & Tell', *NCRC Mission Newsletter* 1.1 (April 2001), p25

74. NCRC, 'Go & Tell', p25

75. Interview with Pastor Pauzie Liegise, Kohima, 2002

76. Angami, *A Brief Account*, p10

77. Ibid, p12

78. NCRC, 'Go & Tell', p26

79. Memorial Service Organizing Committee of His First Death Anniversary, *A Brief Biography of Rev. Neihulie Angami, 1938–2000* (2001), pp6–7

80. Interview with Zhowhuyi of the village of Chesezu, 2002

81. NCRC, 'Go & Tell', p26

82. Memorial Service, *A Brief Biography of Rev. Neihulie Angami*, p7

83. Thong, *Miracles*

84. *Sendenyu Revival Silver Jubilee*, p3

85. Interestingly, this same miracle has occurred in many different places among illiterate people in China during the revival there in recent decades.

86. Thong, *Miracles*, p50

87. *Sendenyu Revival Silver Jubilee*, p5

88. Angami, *A Brief Account*, p15

89. Ibid, p14

90. Hevukhu Achumi Sema, unpublished report

91. CBCNEI Annual Report, 1967, p73

92. Memorial Service, *A Brief Biography of Rev. Neihulie Angami*, p8

93. Philip, *The Growth of Baptist Churches*, p125

94. Memorial Service, *A Brief Biography of Rev. Neihulie Angami*, p10

95. NCRC, 'Go & Tell'

96. Memorial Service, *A Brief Biography of Rev. Neihulie Angami*, pp7–8

97. Angami, *A Brief Account*, p16

98. Dozo, *The Growth of the Baptist Church*, p73

99. Gariphema Christian Revival Church, *The Native Church and Formation of NCRC* (The Literature Committee of the GCRC, 1994), p6

100. Philip, *The Growth of Baptist Churches*, p154

101. Author unknown, 'The Great Revival and Mission Outreach'. In *From Darkness to Light* (Published privately, 1981).

[102.] Memorial Service, *A Brief Biography of Rev. Neihulie Angami*, p4

[103.] Edward Singha, cited in Dozo, *The Growth of the Baptist Church*, p60

[104.] Memorial Service, *A Brief Biography of Rev. Neihulie Angami*, p5

[105.] Dozo, *The Growth of the Baptist Church*, pp59–60

[106.] Interview with Zhowhuyi, 2002

[107.] Dozo, *The Growth of the Baptist Church*, pp19 & 21–23

[108.] Philip, *The Growth of Baptist Churches*, p158

[109.] Angami, *A Brief Account*, pp21–22

[110.] Interview with Pastor Pauzie Liegise, 2002

[111.] Hevukhu Achumi Sema, unpublished report

[112.] 'Through the Border: Voice of the Hidden Peoples', *Ethnos Asia* (April–June 2002)

[113.] India Research Teams, *Peoples of India: Christian Presence and Works among Them* (Chennai: India Missions Association, 1997), p84

[114.] See India Research Teams, *Peoples of India*.

[115.] Some members of the Nagaland Missionary Movement say that the figure of 10,000 referred not to the number of full-time missionaries to be sent out but to a number of people they wanted to 'mobilize for cross-cultural missions', including short-term workers, administrators and intercessors. I am not sure if this is a genuine explanation that was misinterpreted when it was widely reported around the world in the 1970s or a way to save face once it became apparent that the vision had not been realized.

[116.] Hevukhu Achumi Sema, unpublished report

[117.] Kaka D Iralu, *How Then Shall We Live? Reflections on the Political, Economic and Religious Implications of Naga Nationhood* (Kohima: NV Press, 2001), p9

Appendix One

Table of Naga tribes

These statistics refer only to the inhabitants of Nagaland. Several of these tribes have additional members living in other states of north-east India or in Myanmar (Burma). The information comes from India Research Teams, Peoples of India, 1997.

Tribe:	Population (1997)	Christians (1997)	Per cent Christian
Ao	140,000	113,800	81.3
Sumi	134,739	116,228	86.3
Konyak	115,039	114,185	99.3
Angami	86,804	75,125	86.5
Chakhesang	83,572	72,915	87.2
Lotha	79,802	70,075	87.8
Kuki	77,043	54,525	70.8
Phom	34,267	29,779	86.9
Yimchung	30,785	26,886	87.3
Chang	30,769	27,241	88.5
Zeliangrong	28,996	25,208	86.9
Khiamngan	24,863	23,149	93.1
Rengma	21,057	18,668	88.7
TOTAL	887,736	767,804	86.5

APPENDIX TWO

The spread of Christianity in each Naga tribe

This appendix shows statistically how the gospel took root and flourished among the 13 Naga tribes in Nagaland, in chronological order from the Ao, who first received the gospel in 1872, down to the Yimchung, whose first believer was baptized 80 years later in 1952. These figures come from a wide variety of official church sources, books and other documents.

AO NAGA CHURCH MEMBERSHIP (1872–1997)

Year	Members
1872	24
1890	63
1905	685
1920	3,838
1930	9,000
1941	13,776
1961	51,520
1971	58,757
1997	113,800

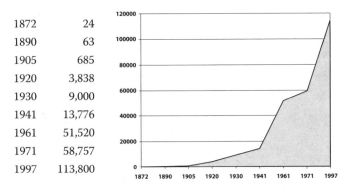

LOTHA NAGA CHURCH MEMBERSHIP (1885–1997)

1885	0
1922	257
1936	1,789
1950	4,000
1955	6,369
1960	8,515
1972	8,647
1976	20,600
1997	70,075

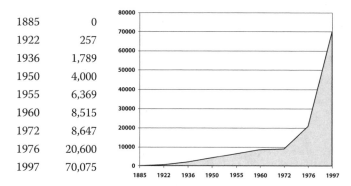

ANGAMI NAGA CHURCH MEMBERSHIP (1886–1997)

1886	4
1914	151
1920	212
1937	630
1950	4,000
1965	6,000
1976	20,000
1997	75,125

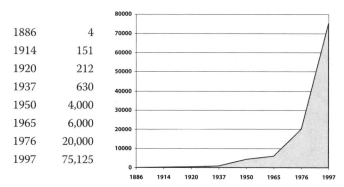

CHAKHESANG NAGA CHURCH MEMBERSHIP (1895–1997)

1895	10
1930	60
1952	700
1956	2,500
1958	8,840
1960	12,144
1971	20,961
1976	25,000
1997	72,915

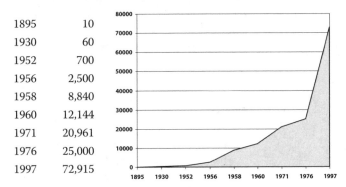

KUKI NAGA CHURCH MEMBERSHIP (1897–1997)

(of the Kuki in Nagaland only)

1897	0
1936	200
1950	700
1958	1,100
1968	1,564
1976	2,800
1997	54,525

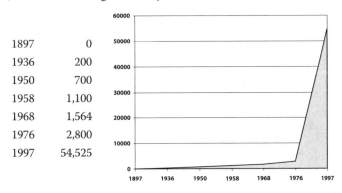

ZELIANGRONG NAGA CHURCH MEMBERSHIP (1905–97)

(in Nagaland only)

1905	0
1951	80
1955	637
1966	1,100
1971	2,000
1976	5,000
1997	25,208

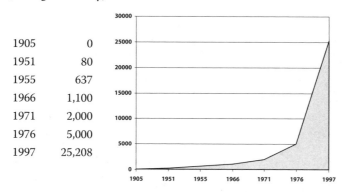

SUMI NAGA CHURCH MEMBERSHIP (1906–97)

1906	0
1929	3,000
1938	8,000
1949	16,000
1962	20,237
1976	41,000
1997	116,228

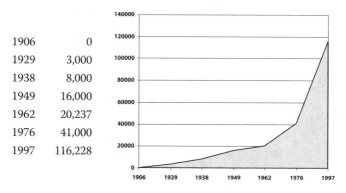

RENGMA NAGA CHURCH MEMBERSHIP (1918–97)

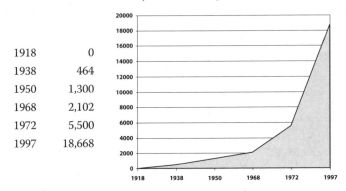

1918	0
1938	464
1950	1,300
1968	2,102
1972	5,500
1997	18,668

KONYAK NAGA CHURCH MEMBERSHIP (1927–97)

(of the Konyak in Nagaland only)

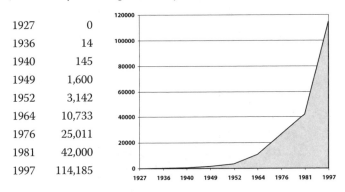

1927	0
1936	14
1940	145
1949	1,600
1952	3,142
1964	10,733
1976	25,011
1981	42,000
1997	114,185

PHOM NAGA CHURCH MEMBERSHIP (1936–97)

1936	0
1952	1,166
1960	3,906
1971	6,000
1979	6,500
1997	29,779

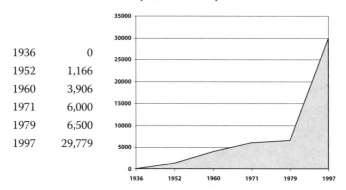

CHANG NAGA CHURCH MEMBERSHIP (1937–97)

1937	0
1947	250
1952	1,573
1955	2,915
1967	4,667
1971	11,901
1997	27,241

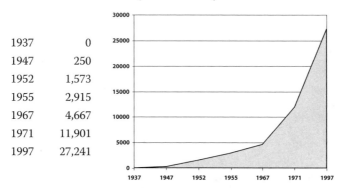

KHIAMNGAN NAGA CHURCH MEMBERSHIP (1950–97)

1950	0
1952	410
1955	538
1960	1,056
1967	5,000
1997	23,149

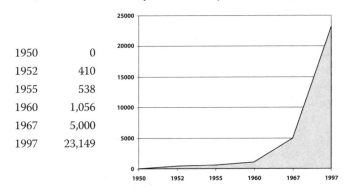

YIMCHUNG NAGA CHURCH MEMBERSHIP (1952–97)

1952	1
1958	500
1963	2,377
1967	5,000
1976	8,301
1997	26,886

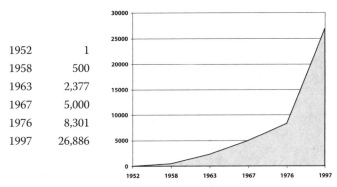

Bibliography

Many of the books and booklets listed below were self-published in Nagaland by churches and individuals interested in recording God's remarkable work among the Nagas. These titles are generally not available outside Nagaland. The author offers his appreciation to those church leaders—and especially Gwayhunlo Khing of Asia Soul Winners—who provided many of these valuable resources to help in the compilation of *From Head-Hunters to Church Planters*.

Aier, N Apokla. 'It Touched All People', in *Tell Out '77: A Focus on Nagaland Revival*. Bombay: Gospel Literature Service, 1977

Alemchiba, M. *A Brief Historical Account of Nagaland*. Kohima: Naga Institute of Culture, 1970

Allen, Louis. *Burma: The Longest War*. London: J M Dent & Sons, 1984

Angami, Neihulie. *A Brief Account of Nagaland Revivals and the Formation of Nagaland Christian Revival Church*. NCRC, 1987

Ao, Bendangyabang A. *History of Christianity in Nagaland: A Source Material*. Mokokchung: Shalom Ministry, 1998

Ao, Kijungluba. 'Molung Church Record'. Typed report, nd

Ao, L Kijung. *Nukinketer Mungchen* [A History of Church Growth in Nagaland]. Gauhati: Christian Literature Centre, nd

Ao, T Alem-meren. *Revival History: Evangelism and Mission*. Mokokchung: Ao CYE Press, nd

Ao, Tajen. *British Occupation of Naga Country*. Kohima: Naga Literature Society, 1993

Ao, Temjen. *Tsungremer Tsunglu* [God's Rain]. Mokokchung: Ao CYE Press, 1979

Aram, M. *Peace in Nagaland: Eight Year Story 1964–1972*. India: Arnold-Heinemann, 1974

Bowers, A C. *Under Head-Hunter's Eyes*. Philadelphia: Judson Press, 1929

Chakhesang Baptist Church Council. *Chakhesang Baptist Kehou Dze* [Brief Account of Chekhesang Baptist Church History] Silver Jubilee 1950–1975. Pfutsero, 1975

Clark, M M. *A Corner in India*. Philadelphia: American Baptist Publication Society, 1907

Colvin, John. *Not Ordinary Men: The Story of the Battle of Kohima.* Barnsley, UK: Pen & Sword, 2004

Dev, S C. *Nagaland: The Untold Story.* Calcutta, 1988

Diran, Richard K. *The Vanishing Tribes of Burma.* London: Weidenfeld & Nicolson, 1997

Downs, F S. *The Mighty Works of God: A Brief History of the Council of Baptist Churches of North East India—the Mission Period 1836–1950.* Gauhati: Christian Literature Centre, 1971

Dozo, Phuveyi. *The Growth of the Baptist Church in Chakhesang Naga Tribe (India).* Pasadena: Fuller Theological Seminary, thesis, 1978

Elwin, Verrier. *Nagaland.* Shillong: P Dutta, 1961

— *Indian North East Frontiers in the Nineteenth Century (sic).* London: Oxford University Press, 1962

— (ed). *The Nagas in the Nineteenth Century.* London: Oxford University Press, 1969

Firth, C B. *An Introduction to Indian Church History.* London: Wesley Press, 1961

Fürer-Haimendorf, Christoph von. *The Naked Nagas.* London: Methuen & Co, 1939

— *The Konyak Nagas.* New York: Holt, Rinehart and Winston, 1969

— *Return to the Naked Nagas: An Anthropologist's View of Nagaland 1936–1976.* New Delhi: Vikas, 1976

Gammell, William. *A History of American Baptist Missions in Asia, Africa, Europe and North America.* Boston: Gould, Kendall and Lincoln, 1850

Gariphema Christian Revival Church. *The Native Church and Formation of NCRC.* The Literature Committee of the GCRC, 1994

Hodson, T K. *The Naga Tribes of Manipur.* London: Macmillan & Co, 1911

Hutton, John Henry. *The Angami Nagas: with Some Notes of the Neighbouring Tribes.* London: Macmillan & Co, 1921

— *The Sema Nagas.* London: Oxford University Press, 1968

India Research Teams. *Peoples of India: Christian Presence and Works among Them.* Chennai: India Missions Association, 1997

Iralu, Kaka D. *Nagaland and India, the Blood and the Tears: A Historical Account of the 52 Years Indo–Naga War and the Story of Those Who Were Never Allowed to Tell It.* Published privately in Nagaland, September 2000

— *How Then Shall We Live? Reflections on the Political, Economic and Religious Implications of Naga Nationhood.* Kohima: NV Press, 2001

King, Christopher R. *The Emergence of Nagaland: A Social and Political Study of Imperial Administration—Missionary Influence and Naga Response.* University of Wisconsin: unpublished thesis, 1969

Longkümer, Akümla. *Revival in Nagaland: Fact or Fallacy?* Mokokchung: Clark Theological College, 1986

Major, V K. *Nagaland in Transition.* New Delhi: Associated Publishing House, 1967

Maxwell, Neville George Anthony. *India and the Nagas.* London: Minority Rights Group, 1973

Memorial Service Organising Committee of His First Death Anniversary. *A Brief Biography of Rev. Neihulie Angami, 1938–2000* (2001)

Merrian, Edmund E. *History of American Baptist Mission.* Philadelphia: American Baptist Publication Society, 1913

Mills, J P. *The Lotha Nagas.* London: Macmillan & Co, 1922

— *The Ao Nagas.* London: Macmillan & Co, 1926

— *The Rengma Nagas.* London: Macmillan & Co, 1937

Morse, Gertrude. *The Dogs May Bark, But the Caravan Moves On.* Published privately by the North Burma Christian Mission, 1998

Nagaland Christian Revival Church. 'Go & Tell'. *NCRC Mission Newsletter* 1.1 (April 2001)

Najekhu, Yepthomi Sema. *A Study of the Growth and Expansion of Baptist Churches in Nagaland with Special Reference to the Major Tribes.* St Paul: Bethel Theological Seminary, unpublished thesis, 1972

Neill, Stephen. *The Story of the Christian Church in India and Pakistan.* Grand Rapids: Eerdmans, 1970

Orr, J Edwin. *Evangelical Awakenings in India.* New Delhi: Masihi Sahitya Santha, 1970

Parakas, Singh. *Nagaland.* New Delhi: National Book Trust, 1972

Philip, Puthuvail Thomas. *The Growth of Baptist Churches in Nagaland.* Gauhati: Christian Literature Centre, 1976

Pickett, J Waskom. *Christian Mass Movements in India.* Lucknow: Lucknow Publishing House, 1933

Podenyi, Pastor. *Chakhesang Revival Christian Church, a Brief Report.* Chesezu Village, Nagaland, 1977

Rao, O M. *Longri Ao: A Biography.* Nagaland, nd

Rikum, Ao. *Nagaland Revival: 1952–*. Mokokchung: Shoppe Press, 1978

Rivenburg, Narola (ed). *The Star of the Naga Hills: Letters from Rev. Sidney and Hattie Rivenburg, Pioneer Missionaries in Assam 1883–1923*. Philadelphia: Judson Press, 1941

Sema, Piketo. *British Policy and Administration in Nagaland 1881–1947*. New Delhi: Scholar Publishing House, 1991

Sendenyu Revival Silver Jubilee: February 1959–February 1984

Shakespear, L W. *History of Upper Assam, Upper Burmah and North-Eastern Frontier*. London: Macmillan & Co, 1914

Singh, K S (ed), *Nagaland. People of India* XXXIV. Calcutta: Seagull Books, 1994

— *The Scheduled Tribes of India. People of India* III. Calcutta: Oxford University Press, 1994

Slim, Field Marshal Sir William. *Defeat into Victory*. London: Four Square Books, 1958

Smith, William Carlson. *The Ao Naga Tribe of Assam: A Study in Ethnology and Sociology*. London: Macmillan & Co, 1925

Stracey, P D. *Nagaland Nightmare*. Bombay: Allied Publishers, 1968

Swinson, Arthur. *The Battle of Kohima*. New York: Stein & Day, 1967

Sword, V H. *Baptists in Assam*. Chicago: Conference Press, 1935

Syiemlieh, David. *A Brief History of the Catholic Church in Nagaland*. Shillong: Vendrame Institute, 1990

Terhuja, Khrieleno. 'A Brief Background of the Church in Nagaland for Organising Committee'. Kohima, Billy Graham Evangelistic Crusade, 1972

'Through the Border: Voice of the Hidden Peoples'. *Ethnos Asia* (April–June 2002)

Thong, Joseph S. *Miracles of the Holy Spirit*. Kohima: Sendenyu Baptist Church, 1995

— *Head-Hunters Culture (Historic Culture of Nagas)*. Tseminyu, Nagaland: Joseph S Thong, 1997

Vasa, Dupor. *The Story of the Naga Gospel Mission to the People of Arunachal Pradesh on the Border of Tibet, China*. India: Arunachal Pradesh Field Mission, 1986

Visor, H. *The Naga Baptist Family*. Kohima: CNBC, 1988

Yaden, L L. *Nagaland*. New Delhi: New Laxmi Press, 1970

Young, Calvin. *The Nagas—An Unknown War*. London, 1962

Zhowhuyi. 'Before and After the Coming of Holy Spirit Fire in Nagaland'. Typed report, Chesezu Village, nd

Paul Hattaway is the director of Asia Harvest,
an organization dedicated to serving the church in Asia.
For more information, visit their website at:
www.asiaharvest.org